100
Delicious
Desserts

100 Delicious Desserts

Edited by
Liza Mostyn

octopus

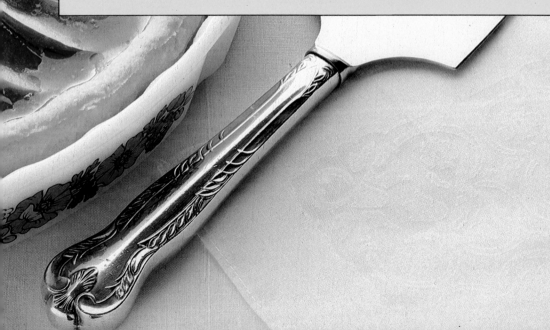

Contents

NOTES
Standard spoon measurements are used in all recipes
1 tablespoon=one 15 ml spoon
1 teaspoon=one 5 ml spoon
All spoon measures are level.

For all recipes, quantities are given in metric, imperial and American measures. Follow one set of measures only, because they are not interchangeable.

First published 1982 by
Octopus Books Limited
59 Grosvenor Street, London W1

© 1982 Octopus Books Limited

ISBN 0 7064 1768 2

Produced by Mandarin Publishers Ltd
22a Westlands Rd
Quarry Bay, Hong Kong

Printed in Hong Kong

Frontispiece: *Toffee Apple Flan (page 40)*
(Photograph: Corning, the manufacturers of Pyrex Glassware)

Introduction

Delicious desserts are often the most favourite part of a meal for everyone concerned – the family and guests enjoy eating them and the cook enjoys cooking them! The 100 recipes here are perfect for all kinds of occasions and they all taste just as good as they look.

One of the most important things about serving desserts is to choose one which complements the rest of the meal. For example, if you are serving a rich main course, then follow it with a refreshing fresh fruit dessert or a light-as-air mousse. On the other hand, if the main course is a light fish or meat dish, then you can easily serve a gorgeous gâteau with lashings of cream, or even a pastry-based dessert such as Chocolate Meringue Pie.

Fruit desserts are a perfect ending to round off a summertime meal. As well as the soft fruits like strawberries and raspberries, don't forget some of the more unusual fruits like avocados, melons and pineapples which can all be turned into some super desserts.

For busy days when you need a quick idea for a pudding, there are lots of recipes for light desserts and cool whips which are all simple – and fast – to make. Then there's a chapter on family puddings for midweek meals. Included here are favourites like trifles and mousses, all kinds of new ideas, plus some special treats the children will love.

It is always a good idea to have a few desserts in the freezer which you can produce with a flourish when an unexpected guest arrives. Pastry freezes well, so we have included a selection of pastry-based ideas. But, of course, the obvious choice for a dessert which can be made well in advance and frozen, is ice cream. Try these new and exciting ices – all with a marvellous texture and flavour to make a happy end to a meal. Honey is used instead of sugar in some of these recipes to give a really delicious flavour and more nutritional value.

At some time almost all of us have to watch our weight. Perhaps the worst thing of all is having to watch others indulge in the most mouthwatering desserts while we content ourselves with an apple or a small piece of cheese. Do not despair – we have included some low calorie recipes as well as some which use only a little sugar or none at all. Try Raspberry Mousse, Strawberry Yogurt Ice or Spicy Apples which are all sure to take your dieting blues away!

The final chapter is a fitting finale to this book as it is full of extra special desserts. They may take a little longer to prepare, but the extra time is well worth it when you see – and taste – the end result! Whether it's for a special dinner party or family celebration, you'll find plenty of delicious ideas to tempt you.

Fruit Desserts

Celebrity Avocado Cocktail

METRIC/IMPERIAL
1 × 225 g/8 oz can
  sliced peaches
2 medium avocados,
  peeled, stoned and
  sliced
225 g/8 oz seedless
  grapes, fresh or
  canned
100 g/4 oz fresh or
  frozen and thawed
  strawberries
1 tablespoon lemon
  juice
1 tablespoon sugar

AMERICAN
1 × 8 oz can sliced
  peaches
2 medium avocados,
  peeled, seeded and
  sliced
½ lb seedless grapes,
  fresh or canned
¼ lb fresh or frozen
  and thawed
  strawberries
1 tablespoon lemon
  juice
1 tablespoon sugar

Drain the peaches and reserve the juice. Combine all the fruits together in a bowl. Blend 300 ml/½ pint (1¼ cups) peach juice with the lemon juice and sugar and pour over the fruits.

Serve chilled in sundae dishes with sweet biscuits (cookies).
Serves 5 to 6

Blackberry Baked Apples

METRIC/IMPERIAL
4 large cooking
  apples, cored
4 slices slimmers'
  bread, crumbed
grated rind and juice
  of 1 orange
pinch of ground
  cinnamon
100 g/4 oz
  blackberries
artificial liquid
  sweetener to taste

AMERICAN
4 large tart apples,
  cored
4 slices slimmers'
  bread, crumbed
grated rind and juice
  of 1 orange
pinch of ground
  cinnamon
¼ lb blackberries
artificial liquid
  sweetener to taste

Score the apple skins around the middle. Mix together the remaining ingredients and fill the cavities of the apples.

Wrap each apple in foil and place them on a baking sheet.

Cook in the centre of a preheated moderately hot oven (190°C/375°F, Gas Mark 5) for 30 to 40 minutes.
Cooking time: 30 to 40 minutes
Serves 4
Note: a good recipe if you are watching your weight as it only has about 135 calories per portion.

Celebrity Avocado Cocktail
(Photograph: Carmel Produce Information Bureau)

Redcurrant Layer Cake

METRIC/IMPERIAL	AMERICAN
100 g/4 oz butter	½ cup butter
100 g/4 oz caster sugar	½ cup sugar
2 eggs, beaten	2 eggs, beaten
100 g/4 oz self-raising flour, sifted	1 cup all-purpose flour, sifted
450 g/1 lb fresh redcurrants	1 lb fresh redcurrants
150 ml/¼ pint double cream	⅔ cup heavy cream
Filling:	**Filling:**
300 ml/½ pint milk	1¼ cups milk
1 vanilla pod	1 vanilla bean
1 egg	1 egg
1 egg yolk	1 egg yolk
50 g/2 oz caster sugar	¼ cup sugar
25 g/1 oz plain flour	¼ cup all-purpose flour

Cream together the butter and sugar. Beat in the eggs. Fold in the flour. Divide the mixture between two greased 18 cm/7 inch sandwich tins (layer cake pans).

Cook in a preheated moderately hot oven (190°C/375°F, Gas Mark 5) for 20 to 25 minutes. Remove the cakes and leave them to cool on a wire rack.

Place the milk and vanilla pod (bean) in a pan, bring to the boil then remove from the heat. Beat the egg and egg yolk with the sugar. Add the flour and beat together. Remove the vanilla pod (bean) from the milk and gradually stir the milk into the egg mixture. Return the custard to the pan and bring to the boil, stirring. Cook for 2 minutes and then leave the custard to cool.

Reserve 100 g/4 oz of the redcurrants for decoration, then crush the remainder.

Whip the cream until just stiff. Cut the cakes in half to make four layers in all. Assemble the cake, spreading some crushed redcurrants and custard filling between each layer. Spread the cream on top and sprinkle with the reserved whole redcurrants.

Cooking time: 30 minutes
Serves 6 to 8

Ogen Sunset Salad

METRIC/IMPERIAL	AMERICAN
1 Ogen melon	1 Ogen melon
3 oranges	3 oranges
225 g/8 oz strawberries	½ lb strawberries
2 teaspoons brandy, sherry or cider	2 teaspoons brandy, sherry or cider
1 tablespoon caster sugar	1 tablespoon sugar

Peel and cut the melon into chunks. Place the melon in a serving bowl. Peel the oranges and cut them into segments. Slice the strawberries and add the oranges and strawberries to the melon. Pour over the brandy, sherry or cider, sprinkle on the sugar and mix well. Chill.
Serves 6

Rice and Orange Mould

METRIC/IMPERIAL	AMERICAN
1 litre/1¾ pints cold milk	4¼ cups cold milk
225 g/8 oz long grain rice	1 cup plus 2 tablespoons long grain rice
2 tablespoons sugar	2 tablespoons sugar
2 tablespoons cornflour	2 tablespoons cornstarch
2 oranges	2 oranges
1 tablespoon powdered gelatine	1 tablespoon unflavored gelatin
50 g/2 oz flaked almonds, toasted	½ cup sliced almonds, toasted

Place 900 ml/1½ pints (3¾ cups) of the milk in a saucepan with the rice and sugar. Bring to the boil and simmer for 30 minutes, stirring occasionally. Mix the cornflour (cornstarch) to a smooth paste with the remaining cold milk. Stir into the rice mixture and leave to cool.

Grate the rind from both oranges and mix it with the juice from 1 orange in a bowl. Stir in the gelatine and heat gently over a pan of simmering water until the gelatine dissolves. Beat the gelatine mixture into the rice. Chop half of the nuts and add them to the rice.

Pour the mixture into a large ring mould and leave to set. Remove the pith from the remaining orange and cut the flesh into slices. Unmould the pudding onto a serving dish and decorate with the orange slices and nuts.

Cooking time: 35 minutes
Serves 6

Berry Trifle Cake

METRIC/IMPERIAL
25 g/1 oz plain flour
1 egg, separated
50 g/2 oz caster sugar
300 ml/½ pint milk
1 sponge flan case
3 tablespoons sherry
   or orange juice
350 g/12 oz
   raspberries,
   strawberries or
   blackberries, or a
   mixture of all three
150 ml/¼ pint double
   cream, whipped
25 g/1 oz icing sugar

AMERICAN
¼ cup all-purpose
   flour
1 egg, separated
¼ cup sugar
1¼ cups milk
1 sponge pie case
3 tablespoons sherry
   or orange juice
¾ lb raspberries,
   strawberries or
   blackberries, or a
   mixture of all three
⅔ cup heavy cream,
   whipped
¼ cup confectioners
   sugar

Beat together the flour, egg yolk, caster sugar and 3 tablespoons of the milk. Pour the remaining milk into a pan and bring to the boil. Pour the milk onto the egg yolk mixture, stir and return to the pan. Bring back to the boil and cook for 1 minute, stirring all the time. Leave on one side to cool.

Whisk the egg white until stiff and fold into the custard.

Place the sponge flan (pie) case on a serving dish. Sprinkle it with the sherry or orange juice. Spoon the custard into the flan (pie) case. Pile the fruit on top.

Spoon the cream into a piping (pastry) bag fitted with a star nozzle and pipe the cream around the top. Sprinkle with the icing (confectioners) sugar.
Serves 6

Jellied Fruit Pudding

METRIC/IMPERIAL
100 g/4 oz sultanas
1 tablespoon currants
100 g/4 oz seedless
   raisins
100 g/4 oz glacé
   cherries
50 g/2 oz chopped
   mixed peel
150 ml/¼ pint sherry
1 tablespoon brandy
150 ml/¼ pint water
4 tablespoons sugar
1 piece lemon rind
2 tablespoons lemon
   juice
3 teaspoons
   powdered gelatine
25 g/1 oz shredded
   almonds

AMERICAN
1½ cups golden
   raisins
1 tablespoon currants
½ cup glacé cherries
⅓ cup chopped
   candied peel
⅔ cup sherry
1 tablespoon brandy
⅔ cup water
4 tablespoons sugar
1 piece lemon rind
2 tablespoons lemon
   juice
3 teaspoons
   unflavored gelatin
¼ cup sliced almonds

Cook the sultanas (golden raisins), currants and raisins in a little hot water for 15 minutes until plump. Strain.

Slice the cherries and add them to the fruit with the chopped peel. Pour over the sherry and brandy and cover.

Put the water in a pan with the sugar, lemon rind and juice. Bring slowly to the boil and strain. Add the gelatine and stir until dissolved. Add sufficient cold water to make up to 300 ml/½ pint (1¼ cups). Pour over the fruit and fold in the almonds.

Pour the mixture into a 900 ml/1½ pint (3¾ cup) mould or basin and chill.

Unmould on a serving dish and serve with cream or ice cream.
Cooking time: 20 minutes
Serves 6

Avocado Orange Cheesecake

METRIC/IMPERIAL

175 g/6 oz digestive biscuits, crushed
50 g/2 oz butter, melted
1 ripe avocado, peeled and stoned
75 g/3 oz cream cheese
150 ml/¼ pint soured cream
4 teaspoons lemon juice
finely grated rind of ½ orange
2-3 tablespoons caster sugar
1½ teaspoons powdered gelatine
1 tablespoon hot water
1 egg white
1 orange, peeled and cut into segments

AMERICAN

2¼ cups graham cracker crumbs
¼ cup butter, melted
1 ripe avocado, peeled and seeded
⅓ cup cream cheese
⅔ cup sour cream
4 teaspoons lemon juice
finely grated rind of ½ orange
2-3 tablespoons sugar
1½ teaspoons unflavored gelatin
1 tablespoon hot water
1 egg white
1 orange, peeled and cut into segments

Mix the biscuit (cracker) crumbs with the butter until evenly coated, then press into the bottom of an 18 cm/7 inch lightly greased flan (pie) ring. Chill until set.

Mash three-quarters of the avocado and beat in the cheese, sour cream and 3 teaspoons lemon juice until smooth. Add the orange rind and sugar to taste.

Place the gelatine in a small bowl with the hot water and stir until it has dissolved; leave to cool. Stir the gelatine into the avocado mixture. Whisk the egg white until stiff and fold into the mixture. Pour onto the crumb base and chill until set.

Remove the flan (pie) ring. Just before serving, decorate with the orange segments and remaining slices of the avocado dipped in lemon juice.
Serves 6 to 8

Spiced Fruit Compote

METRIC/IMPERIAL

1 × 275 g/10 oz can pear quarters in fruit juice
1 × 425 g/15 oz can pineapple rings in natural juice
1 × 275 g/10 oz can apricot halves in fruit juice
1 × 290 g/10½ oz can mandarin orange segments in natural juice
6 cloves
1 cinnamon stick, broken into 4 pieces
150 ml/¼ pint sweet white wine
100 g/4 oz fresh or frozen and thawed raspberries

AMERICAN

1 × 10 oz can pear quarters in fruit juice
1 × 15 oz can pineapple rings in natural juice
1 × 10 oz can apricot halves in fruit juice
1 × 10½ oz can mandarin orange segments in natural juice
6 cloves
1 cinnamon stick, broken into 4 pieces
⅔ cup sweet white wine
¼ lb fresh or frozen and thawed raspberries

Drain the fruit, reserving all the juice, and cut the pineapple rings in half. Arrange the fruit in a large bowl.

Place the fruit juice, cloves and cinnamon stick in a pan, bring to the boil and boil rapidly for 5 minutes. Add the wine and boil rapidly for a further 5 minutes. Pour over the fruit and leave to go cold.

Just before serving, pour the fruit and juice mixture into a glass serving bowl and carefully stir in the raspberries.
Cooking time: 15 minutes
Serves 6 to 8

Spiced Fruit Compote
(Photograph: John West Foods Limited)

Avocado and Pineapple Flan

METRIC/IMPERIAL	AMERICAN
Pastry:	**Pastry:**
175 g/6 oz plain flour	1½ cups all-purpose
75 g/3 oz butter or	flour
margarine	6 tablespoons butter
1-2 tablespoons iced	or shortening
water	1-2 tablespoons iced
Filling:	water
1 × 225 g/8 oz can	**Filling:**
pineapple	1 × 8 oz can
1½ teaspoons	pineapple
powdered gelatine	1½ teaspoons
2 tablespoons caster	unflavored gelatin
sugar	2 tablespoons sugar
1 large ripe avocado	1 large ripe avocado
1 tablespoon lemon	1 tablespoon lemon
juice	juice
150 ml/¼ pint double	⅔ cup heavy cream
cream	

Sift the flour into a bowl and rub (cut) in the fat until the mixture resembles fine breadcrumbs. Add the water gradually and mix to a firm dough. Roll out the dough and use to line a 20 cm/8 inch fluted flan (pie) ring. Line with greaseproof (waxed) paper and dried beans and cook in a preheated moderately hot oven (200°C/400°F, Gas Mark 6) for 15 to 20 minutes. Remove paper and beans and return flan to the oven for 5 minutes. Cool completely on a wire rack and remove flan (pie) ring.

Drain the pineapple and make the juice up to 150 ml/¼ pint (⅔ cup) with water if necessary. Sprinkle the gelatine over the juice in a bowl and leave to soak. Place the bowl over a pan of simmering water and stir until the gelatine has dissolved. Add the sugar, stir until dissolved then leave to cool.

Chop the pineapple. Peel and chop the avocado and mix with the lemon juice and pineapple. Place the fruit in the baked flan (pie) case. Whip half the cream until thick. When the gelatine mixture is on the point of setting, fold in the whipped cream and spoon it over the pineapple and avocado. Chill until set.

Whip the remaining cream and use to decorate the flan.
Cooking time: 25 minutes
Serves 6

Melon Cheesecake

METRIC/IMPERIAL	AMERICAN
50 g/2 oz butter	¼ cup butter
1 tablespoon golden	1 tablespoon corn
syrup	syrup
175 g/6 oz digestive	2¼ cups graham
biscuits, crushed	cracker crumbs
225 g/8 oz cream	1 cup cream cheese
cheese	⅔ cup plain yogurt
150 ml/¼ pint plain	2 tablespoons ginger
yogurt	or orange
2 tablespoons ginger	marmalade
or orange	1 egg yolk
marmalade	2 teaspoons
1 egg yolk	unflavored gelatin
2 teaspoons	2 tablespoons orange
powdered gelatine	juice
2 tablespoons orange	2 egg whites
juice	2 tablespoons sugar
2 egg whites	1 Ogen or Galia
2 tablespoons caster	melon
sugar	
1 Ogen or Galia	
melon	

Heat the butter and syrup gently until melted. Stir in the biscuit (cracker) crumbs until well coated. Press into the bottom of a greased deep 20 cm/8 inch loose-bottomed cake tin (spring-form pan) and chill until firm.

Beat the cream cheese until smooth then beat in the yogurt. Beat in the marmalade and egg yolk.

Dissolve the gelatine in the orange juice in a small bowl over a pan of simmering water. Leave to cool then stir the gelatine into the cream cheese mixture.

Whisk the egg whites until stiff then whisk in the sugar. Fold into the cheese mixture and pour over the crumb base. Chill until set.

To serve, carefully remove from the tin to a serving plate and decorate the top with slices and/or balls of melon.
Serves 6 to 8

Honeycomb Fruit Ring

METRIC/IMPERIAL	AMERICAN
1 tablespoon powdered gelatine	1 tablespoon unflavored gelatin
4 tablespoons hot water	4 tablespoons hot water
2 large eggs, separated	2 large eggs, separated
50 g/2 oz sugar	¼ cup sugar
600 ml/1 pint milk	2½ cups milk
few drops vanilla essence	few drops vanilla extract
225 g/8 oz soft fruit in season	½ lb soft fruit in season

Place the gelatine in a small bowl with the hot water and stir until it has dissolved. Leave to cool but not set.

Beat the egg yolks and sugar together in a heatproof bowl. Bring the milk to the boil in a pan and pour onto the egg yolks. Place the bowl over a pan of simmering water and cook, stirring occasionally, until the custard thickens slightly. Stir in the gelatine and vanilla. Leave to cool.

Whisk the egg whites until very stiff. When the custard mixture is cool but not set, fold in the egg whites. Pour into a 1.2 litre/2 pint (5 cup) ring mould. Chill until firmly set.

Dip the mould quickly in hot water and unmould on a serving dish. Fill the centre with soft fruit such as blackberries, raspberries, blackcurrants, etc.
Serves 4 to 6

Tropicana

METRIC/IMPERIAL	AMERICAN
5 teaspoons powdered gelatine	5 teaspoons unflavored gelatin
120 ml/4 fl oz hot water	½ cup hot water
450 ml/¾ pint ginger ale	2 cups ginger ale
4 tablespoons lemon juice	4 tablespoons lemon juice
450 g/1 lb fresh fruit, diced or sliced (strawberries, peaches, apricots, cherries, pears, pineapple)	1 lb fresh fruit, diced or sliced (strawberries, peaches, apricots, cherries, pears, pineapple)

Place the gelatine in a bowl with the hot water and stir until it has dissolved. Gradually add the ginger ale and lemon juice. Allow the froth to subside then remove some of the excess froth.

Pour into a 1.75 litre/3 pint (2 quart) mould and leave until syrupy. Spoon the fruit salad into the mould and chill until firm. Unmould on a serving dish and serve with cream.
Serves 6

Sunset Oranges

METRIC/IMPERIAL	AMERICAN
6 oranges	6 oranges
6 tablespoons granulated sugar	6 tablespoons sugar
150 ml/¼ pint ginger cordial	⅔ cup ginger cordial

Thinly pare the rind from 1 orange. Cut the rind into thin strips, place them in a pan and cover with water. Boil for 5 minutes. Rinse them under cold water, drain and leave on one side.

Cut the peel and white pith off all the oranges and slice them neatly into a dish.

Place the sugar and half the cordial into a heavy-based pan and dissolve the sugar over a gentle heat. When it is clear, boil rapidly so that the syrup darkens and thickens. Remove the pan from the heat and carefully pour in the remaining cordial which will bubble furiously. Return the pan to the heat and stir until the caramel has dissolved.

Cool the syrup, then pour it over the orange slices and scatter the orange rind strips on top. Serve chilled.
Serves 4 to 6

Melon and Strawberries in Cointreau

METRIC/IMPERIAL	AMERICAN
1 Galia or Ogen melon	1 Galia or Ogen melon
450 g/1 lb strawberries, hulled	1 lb strawberries, hulled
3 tablespoons Cointreau	3 tablespoons Cointreau
fresh mint leaves to decorate	fresh mint leaves to decorate
150 ml/¼ pint double cream, lightly whipped	⅔ cup heavy cream, lightly whipped

Cut the melon in half, zig-zagging the edges, and discard the seeds. Scoop out the flesh with a melon baller. Cut out any remaining melon flesh and chop. Toss the melon balls and strawberries together with the Cointreau.

Place the melon halves in two individual dishes and spoon the roughly chopped melon into the base. Arrange the melon balls and strawberries on top.

Decorate with mint and serve lightly chilled with whipped cream.
Serves 2

Spicy Apples

METRIC/IMPERIAL	AMERICAN
4 red dessert apples, cored and sliced	4 red-skinned apples, cored and sliced
½ teaspoon nutmeg	½ teaspoon nutmeg
1 cinnamon stick	1 cinnamon stick
rind of ½ lemon, cut into thin lengths	rind of ½ lemon, cut into thin lengths
300 ml/½ pint water	1¼ cups water
3 tablespoons low calorie orange squash	3 tablespoons low calorie orange drink

Place the apples in a pan with the spices, lemon rind and water.

Bring to the boil and then remove from the heat. Stir in the orange squash (drink) and chill thoroughly.

Serve with low fat yogurt if desired.
Serves 4

Note: a good recipe if you are watching your weight as it only contains about 60 calories per portion.

Spicy Apples
(Photograph: Outline Slimming Bureau)

Lemon and Orange Pudding

METRIC/IMPERIAL	AMERICAN
25 g/1 oz butter	2 tablespoons butter
100 g/4 oz caster sugar	½ cup sugar
grated rind and juice of 1 large lemon	grated rind and juice of 1 large lemon
2 eggs, separated	2 eggs, separated
50 g/2 oz self-raising flour, sifted	½ cup all-purpose flour, sifted
150 ml/¼ pint milk	⅔ cup milk
2 small oranges, peeled and thinly sliced	2 small oranges, peeled and thinly sliced
icing sugar for sprinkling	confectioners sugar for sprinkling

Place the butter, sugar and lemon rind into a basin and cream together. Beat in the egg yolks. Add the sifted flour and milk. (The mixture will look curdled.)

Add the lemon juice and mix well. Whisk the egg whites to soft peaks and fold into the mixture, mixing well.

Pour into a greased ovenproof dish. Stand the dish in a roasting pan, containing 2.5 cm/1 inch warm water. Cook in a preheated moderately hot oven (190°C/375°F, Gas Mark 5) for 35 to 40 minutes.

Top the dessert with sliced oranges and sprinkle with icing (confectioners) sugar.
Cooking time: 35 to 40 minutes
Serves 4

Syllabub Sundae

METRIC/IMPERIAL	AMERICAN
1 egg white	1 egg white
50 g/2 oz caster sugar	¼ cup sugar
¼ teaspoon grated lemon rind	¼ teaspoon grated lemon rind
2 teaspoons lemon juice	2 teaspoons lemon juice
4 tablespoons dry white wine	4 tablespoons dry white wine
150 ml/¼ pint double cream	⅔ cup heavy cream
¼ watermelon or an Ogen melon	¼ small watermelon or an Ogen melon
4-6 digestive biscuits, crushed	4-6 graham crackers, crushed

Whisk the egg white until stiff and fold in the sugar, lemon rind and juice and wine. Whip the cream until thick but not too stiff and fold into the lemon mixture.

Cut the melon into small cubes or balls, discarding all the seeds. Fill four tall glasses with layers of melon, syllabub, crumbs and finally more syllabub on top.

Decorate each one with a piece of melon.
Serves 4

Lemon Meringue Puffs

METRIC/IMPERIAL	AMERICAN
4 eggs, separated	4 eggs, separated
artificial sweetener to taste	artificial sweetener to taste
finely grated rind of ½ lemon	finely grated rind of ½ lemon
4 tablespoons 1-calorie lemonade	4 tablespoons 1-calorie lemonade

Whisk the egg whites until stiff and add the artificial sweetener. Spoon or pipe the meringue into 8 rounds on a baking sheet lined with non-stick paper (parchment). Cook in a preheated very cool oven (110°C/225°F, Gas Mark ¼) for 1 hour. Place on a serving dish.

Whisk the egg yolks, lemon rind and lemonade in a basin over hot water until thick and frothy. Pour over the meringues and serve.
Cooking time: 1 hour
Serves 4
Note: a good recipe if you are watching your weight as it only contains about 66 calories per portion.

Danish Apple Dessert

METRIC/IMPERIAL	AMERICAN
750 g/1½ lb cooking apples	1½ lb tart apples
75 g/3 oz butter	6 tablespoons butter
100 g/4 oz fresh white breadcrumbs	2 cups soft white bread crumbs
6 tablespoons sugar	6 tablespoons sugar
150 ml/¼ pint whipping cream	⅔ cup whipping cream

Peel, core and slice the apples and cook them slowly with just enough water to cover the bottom of the pan. When soft, mash the apples to a purée with a fork, adding 25 g/1 oz (2 tablespoons) of the butter and some sugar to taste if liked. Leave to cool.

Melt the remaining butter in a frying pan, add the breadcrumbs and sugar and fry until golden brown and crisp, turning frequently. Leave to cool.

Just before serving, arrange alternate layers of apples and crumbs in a glass bowl, finishing with a layer of crumbs. Decorate with the whipped cream.
Cooking time: 25 minutes
Serves 4

Cherry Cheesecake

METRIC/IMPERIAL	AMERICAN
50 g/2 oz butter	¼ cup butter
100 g/4 oz digestive biscuits, crushed	1½ cups graham cracker crumbs
50 g/2 oz caster sugar	¼ cup sugar
3 teaspoons powdered gelatine	3 teaspoons unflavored gelatin
3 tablespoons water	3 tablespoons water
225 g/8 oz cottage cheese	1 cup cottage cheese
50 g/2 oz sifted icing sugar	½ cup sifted confectioners sugar
150 ml/¼ pint double cream	⅔ cup heavy cream
1 teaspoon grated lemon rind	1 teaspoon grated lemon rind
1 tablespoon lemon juice	1 tablespoon lemon juice
150 ml/¼ pint milk	⅔ cup milk
1 × 450 g/15 oz can stoned cherries	1 × 16 oz can pitted cherries
1 tablespoon cornflour	1 tablespoon cornstarch

Melt the butter in a pan and mix in the biscuit (cracker) crumbs and caster sugar. Press into the bottom of an 18 cm/7 inch loose-bottomed cake tin (springform pan). Sprinkle the gelatine over the water in a small bowl. Cream the cottage cheese and icing (confectioners) sugar together. Lightly whip the cream and add to the cottage cheese mixture with the lemon rind and juice.

Place the gelatine in the bowl over a pan of simmering water and stir until dissolved. Stir into the cottage cheese mixture. Stir in the milk and pour over the crumb base. Chill until firmly set. Ease a knife around the edge of the cheesecake and transfer to a serving dish.

Drain the cherries, reserving the juice. Arrange the cherries over the cheesecake.

Mix the cornflour (cornstarch) to a smooth paste with a little of the cherry juice. Bring the rest of the juice to the boil and pour onto the cornflour (cornstarch). Return to the pan, bring back to the boil and cook for 1 minute until thickened. Leave to cool. Spoon the glaze over the cherries and leave until cold.
Serves 6
Variation:
Omit the cherry topping and instead purée 225 g/8 oz (½ cup) raspberries and add icing (confectioners) sugar to taste. Pipe whipped cream around top of cheesecake and serve the raspberry sauce separately.

Quick & Easy Desserts

Rosy Apples

METRIC/IMPERIAL
750 g/1½ lb cooking apples
150 ml/¼ pint blackcurrant flavour cordial
2 teaspoons powdered gelatine
3 tablespoons hot water
50 g/2 oz dried milk powder
150 ml/¼ pint plain yogurt

AMERICAN
1½ lb apples
⅔ cup blackcurrant flavor cordial
2 teaspoons unflavored gelatin
3 tablespoons hot water
⅔ cup dried milk powder
⅔ cup plain yogurt

Peel, core and slice the apples then simmer in the cordial until soft. Sieve or purée the apples in a blender or food processor.

Place the gelatine in a small bowl with the hot water and stir until it has dissolved. Pour the gelatine in a steady stream into the apple purée, stirring well. Leave to cool.

Make up the dried milk to 300 ml/½ pint (1¼ cups) with water and stir into the apple. When the mixture is beginning to set, spoon into four glasses and swirl the yogurt on top.
Serves 4

Raspberry Ripple Glory

METRIC/IMPERIAL
450 g/1 lb fresh or frozen and thawed raspberries
6 tablespoons raspberry jam
8 scoops raspberry ripple ice cream
150 ml/¼ pint double cream, whipped
chopped walnuts

AMERICAN
1 lb fresh or frozen and thawed raspberries
6 tablespoons raspberry jam
8 scoops raspberry ripple ice cream
⅔ cup heavy cream, whipped
chopped walnuts

Reserve a few raspberries for decoration and mix the rest with the jam. Divide half the fruit mixture between four tall glasses. Add one scoop of ice cream to each glass and top with the whipped cream. Add the remaining fruit mixture and top with the remaining ice cream.

Decorate with the reserved raspberries and chopped walnuts.
Serves 4

Rosy Apples
(Photograph: Cadbury Typhoo Food Advisory Service)

19

Pineapple and Orange Whip

METRIC/IMPERIAL
1 × 425 g/15 oz can
  pineapple rings in
  natural juice
grated rind and juice
  of 1 medium
  orange
1 tablespoon
  powdered gelatine
2 egg whites
50 g/2 oz caster sugar
whipped cream to
  decorate

AMERICAN
1 × 15 oz can
  pineapple rings in
  natural juice
grated rind and juice
  of 1 medium
  orange
1 tablespoon
  unflavored gelatin
2 egg whites
¼ cup sugar
whipped cream to
  decorate

Drain the pineapple rings, reserving the juice. Roughly chop the fruit, place in a blender or food processor with the juice and half the orange rind and blend to a thick purée.

Sprinkle the gelatine over the orange juice in a small bowl. Place the bowl over a pan of simmering water and stir until dissolved. Leave to cool. Stir the gelatine into the pineapple purée and chill until just on the point of setting.

Meanwhile whisk the egg whites until they form soft peaks. Add the sugar and continue whisking until well blended. Fold the egg whites into the pineapple mixture. Spoon into individual glass dishes and chill until set.

Decorate with whipped cream and the remaining orange rind.
Serves 4

Lemon Cheese

METRIC/IMPERIAL
175 g/6 oz cream
  cheese
50 g/2 oz caster sugar
grated rind and juice
  of ½ lemon
2 eggs, separated
150 ml/¼ pint double
  cream, whipped
grated nutmeg to
  decorate

AMERICAN
¾ cup cream cheese
¼ cup sugar
grated rind and juice
  of ½ lemon
2 eggs, separated
⅔ cup heavy cream,
  whipped
grated nutmeg to
  decorate

Beat the cream cheese and sugar together until smooth and creamy. Add the lemon rind and juice and egg yolks and mix well.

Whisk the egg whites until fairly stiff. Fold the cream and egg whites into the mixture.

Pour into four glass dishes and chill. Decorate with the nutmeg before serving.
Serves 4

Butterscotch Crunch Parfait

METRIC/IMPERIAL
50 g/2 oz cornflakes
50 g/2 oz butter
50 g/2 oz soft brown
  sugar
300 ml/½ pint plain
  yogurt
a little whipped cream
  to decorate

AMERICAN
2 cups cornflakes
¼ cup butter
⅓ cup soft brown
  sugar
1¼ cups plain yogurt
a little whipped cream
  to decorate

Crush the cornflakes finely with a rolling pin. Melt the butter and sugar together in a heavy pan and boil gently for a few seconds. Stir in the cornflakes.

Just before serving, put a spoonful of the yogurt in the bottom of four glasses then a layer of the cornflake mixture and another layer of yogurt. Continue layering the yogurt and cornflake mixture in this way, reserving a little of the cornflake mixture; finish with a layer of yogurt.

Decorate with a little whipped cream and sprinkle with the reserved cornflake mixture. Serve chilled.
Serves 4

Zabaglione Tosca

METRIC/IMPERIAL
6 egg yolks
100 g/4 oz sugar
2 teaspoons
  powdered gelatine
120 ml/4 fl oz hot
  water
175 ml/6 fl oz Marsala
4 tablespoons brandy
250 ml/8 fl oz
  whipped cream
5 egg whites
whipped cream to
  decorate

AMERICAN
6 egg yolks
½ cup sugar
2 teaspoons
  unflavored gelatin
½ cup hot water
¾ cup Marsala
4 tablespoons brandy
1 cup whipped cream
5 egg whites
whipped cream to
  decorate

Beat the egg yolks and sugar until creamy. Sprinkle the gelatine over the hot water in a bowl and stir until dissolved. Stir the gelatine into the egg mixture. Gradually add the Marsala, brandy and whipped cream, mixing thoroughly together.

Beat the egg whites until stiff but not dry and fold them into the mixture. Pour into glasses and refrigerate.

Decorate with whipped cream.
Serves 6 to 8

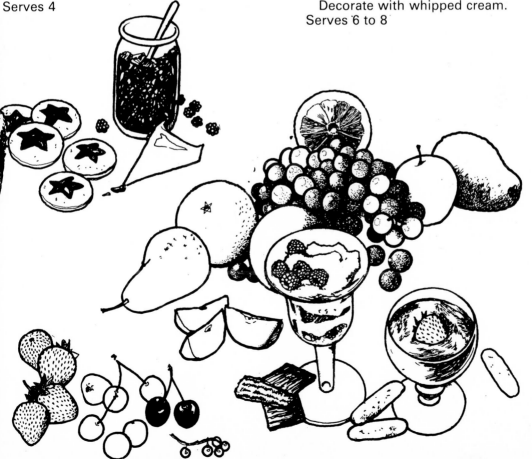

Apple and Blackcurrant Fluff

METRIC/IMPERIAL	AMERICAN
450 g/1 lb cooking apples	1 lb tart apples
4 tablespoons water	4 tablespoons water
sugar to taste	sugar to taste
2 egg whites	2 egg whites
2 tablespoons blackcurrant jam	2 tablespoons blackcurrant jam

Peel, core and slice the apples. Cook them in the water with sugar to taste to a thick pulp. Leave to cool.

Whisk the egg whites until stiff and fold gently into the apple purée.

Spoon into four individual glass dishes and swirl the jam on top.

Cooking time: 15 minutes

Serves 4

Shimmering Cloud

METRIC/IMPERIAL	AMERICAN
1 packet raspberry jelly	1 package raspberry-flavored gelatin
300 ml/½ pint raspberry yogurt	1¼ cups raspberry yogurt

Make up the jelly (gelatin) as directed on the packet and leave to cool.

Sieve the yogurt to remove the raspberry seeds. Stir or whisk the yogurt into the jelly (gelatin) until well blended.

Pour into a rinsed 900 ml/1½ pint (3¾ cup) mould and leave to set. Unmould the dessert on a serving plate.

Serves 4 to 6

Cointreau and Mandarin Mousse

METRIC/IMPERIAL	AMERICAN
1 × 290 g/10½ oz can mandarin orange segments in natural juice	1 × 10½ oz can mandarin orange segments in natural juice
1 tablespoon powdered gelatine	1 tablespoon unflavored gelatin
4 tablespoons Cointreau	4 tablespoons Cointreau
3 egg yolks	3 egg yolks
2 tablespoons caster sugar	2 tablespoons sugar

Drain the juice from the mandarin oranges into a large heatproof bowl. Sprinkle the gelatine over the juice.

Pour 2 tablespoons Cointreau over the oranges and leave to soak. Add the remaining Cointreau, egg yolks and sugar to the gelatine. Place the bowl over hot but not boiling water and whisk with an electric mixer for about 3 to 4 minutes, until very thick and foamy.

Pour into six individual glass dishes and chill until set.

Spoon the soaked mandarin orange segments on top.

Serves 6

Cointreau and Mandarin Mousse
(Photograph: John West Foods Limited)

Watermelon Meringues

METRIC/IMPERIAL	AMERICAN
½ small watermelon	½ small watermelon
a little crushed mint	a little crushed mint
4-6 individual meringue nests	4-6 individual meringue nests
frosted mint leaves to decorate	frosted mint leaves to decorate

Scoop out the melon into balls, discarding the seeds and place in a bowl with a little crushed mint. Just before serving, spoon the drained melon balls into the meringue nests and decorate with frosted mint.

To frost mint: dip the leaves or small sprigs of fresh mint into lightly beaten egg white and then coat with caster sugar. Leave to dry.
Serves 4 to 6

Strawberry Banana Bavarian

METRIC/IMPERIAL	AMERICAN
1 packet strawberry jelly	1 package strawberry-flavored gelatin
120 ml/4 fl oz double cream, whipped	½ cup heavy cream, whipped
4 ripe bananas, sliced	4 ripe bananas, sliced

Make up the jelly (gelatin) following the directions on the packet and leave until almost set. Fold in the whipped cream.

Fill six glasses with alternate layers of the jelly (gelatin) mixture and the sliced bananas. Chill until set.
Serves 6

Raspberry Mousse

METRIC/IMPERIAL	AMERICAN
225 g/8 oz raspberries	½ lb raspberries
1 tablespoon low calorie spread	1 tablespoon low calorie margarine
1 teaspoon lemon juice	1 teaspoon lemon juice
1 tablespoon powdered gelatine	1 tablespoon unflavored gelatin
1 tablespoon hot water	1 tablespoon hot water
150 ml/¼ pint plain low fat yogurt	⅔ cup plain low fat yogurt
1 egg white	1 egg white
raspberries to decorate	raspberries to decorate

Cook the raspberries with the low calorie spread (margarine) and lemon juice until they form a pulp. Remove from the heat and sieve.

Sprinkle the gelatine over the hot water in a bowl and stir until dissolved. Leave to cool slightly, then stir the gelatine and yogurt into the raspberry purée.

When the mixture is on the point of setting, whisk the egg white until just stiff and fold it in.

Pour the mousse into a 600 ml/1 pint (2½ cup) mould and leave to set. Unmould on a serving plate and decorate with a few whole raspberries.
Serves 4

Note: a good recipe if you are watching your weight as it only contains about 60 calories per portion.

Blackcurrant Creams

METRIC/IMPERIAL	AMERICAN
4 tablespoons blackcurrant cordial	4 tablespoons blackcurrant cordial
100 g/4 oz caster sugar	½ cup sugar
40 g/1½ oz cornflour	6 tablespoons cornstarch
40 g/1½ oz butter	3 tablespoons butter
150 ml/¼ pint milk	⅔ cup milk
2 eggs, separated	2 eggs, separated
150 ml/¼ pint plain yogurt	⅔ cup plain yogurt
2 tablespoons cornflakes	2 tablespoons cornflakes

In a pan whisk together the blackcurrant cordial, sugar, cornflour (cornstarch), butter and milk. Heat until smooth and boiling and cook for a few minutes. Leave to cool slightly and beat in the egg yolks.

Leave to cool completely then stir in the yogurt. Beat the egg whites until stiff and fold into the yogurt mixture. Divide between four dishes or glasses and chill. Sprinkle a few cornflakes on each dessert just before serving. Serve immediately.
Serves 4

Lemon Whip

METRIC/IMPERIAL	AMERICAN
½ packet lemon jelly	½ package lemon-flavored gelatin
grated rind and juice of 1 lemon	grated rind and juice of 1 lemon
2 egg whites	2 egg whites
1 tablespoon caster sugar	1 tablespoon sugar
150 ml/¼ pint double cream	⅔ cup heavy cream
5 lemon slices to decorate	5 lemon slices to decorate

Dissolve the lemon jelly (gelatin) in 150 ml/¼ pint (⅔ cup) boiling water. Add the lemon rind and juice and make up to 300 ml/½ pint (1¼ cups) with cold water. Leave in a cold place until just on the point of setting.

Whisk the egg whites until very stiff and fold into the jelly (gelatin) with the sugar. Whip cream lightly and fold into the lemon mixture. Spoon into five tall glasses and decorate with lemon slices.
Serves 5

Family Desserts

Harlequin Peach Trifle

METRIC/IMPERIAL	AMERICAN
1 battenburg cake	1 battenburg cake
1 packet lemon or peach jelly	1 package lemon or peach-flavored gelatin
150 ml/¼ pint boiling water	⅔ cup boiling water
2 × 275 g/10 oz cans peach slices in fruit juice	2 × 10 oz cans peach slices in fruit juice
3 tablespoons custard powder	3 tablespoons Bird's English Dessert Mix
2 tablespoons sugar	2 tablespoons sugar
600 ml/1 pint milk	2½ cups milk
300 ml/½ pint double cream	1¼ cups heavy cream
angelica to decorate	angelica to decorate

Slice the cake and arrange the slices in the bottom of a glass dish. Dissolve the jelly (gelatin) in the water and leave to cool.

Drain the juice from the cans of peaches and make up to 300 ml/½ pint (1¼ cups) with water. Stir into the jelly (gelatin), then chill until the consistency of unbeaten egg white. Spoon the jelly (gelatin) over the cake and leave to set.

Meanwhile reserve 16 peach slices for decoration. Slice the remaining peach slices in half and lay on top of the jelly (gelatin).

Make up the custard (Dessert Mix) in the usual way with the sugar and milk. Leave to cool then spoon on top of the peaches. Chill until completely cold.

Whip the cream until it holds its shape and spread on top of the custard. Decorate with the reserved peach slices and diamond shaped pieces of angelica. Chill until ready to serve.
Serves 8

Harlequin Peach Trifle
(Photograph: John West Foods Limited)

Coffee and Ginger Soufflé

METRIC/IMPERIAL	AMERICAN
1 tablespoon powdered gelatine	1 tablespoon unflavored gelatin
3 tablespoons hot water	3 tablespoons hot water
150 ml/¼ pint double cream	⅔ cup heavy cream
100 g/4 oz caster sugar	½ cup sugar
4 eggs, separated	4 eggs, separated
2 tablespoons sliced stem ginger	2 tablespoons sliced preserved ginger
2 tablespoons syrup from the stem ginger	2 tablespoons syrup from the preserved ginger
3 tablespoons strong black coffee	3 tablespoons strong black coffee
To decorate:	**To decorate:**
a little whipped cream	a little whipped cream
a few slices stem ginger	a few slices preserved ginger

Tie a double band of greaseproof (waxed) paper around a 600 ml/1 pint (2½ cup) soufflé dish to stand 5 cm/2 inches above the rim; oil the inside of the paper.

Place the gelatine in a small bowl with the hot water and stir until it has dissolved.

Whip the cream until just thick. Add the sugar to the egg yolks and whisk until thick and creamy. Add the ginger, syrup and coffee to the egg mixture. Pour in the gelatine in a steady stream, whisking all the time. Fold the cream into the mixture.

Whisk the egg whites fairly stiffly and fold in. Pour the mixture into the soufflé dish and leave until cold and set.

When set, carefully peel away the paper with a knife. Decorate with a little whipped cream and a few slices of ginger.
Serves 6

Banana and Chocolate Trifle

METRIC/IMPERIAL	AMERICAN
1 packet pineapple jelly	1 package pineapple-flavored gelatin
3 bananas	3 bananas
1 chocolate Swiss roll	1 chocolate jelly roll
2 tablespoons cocoa powder	2 tablespoons unsweetened cocoa
1 tablespoon cornflour	1 tablespoon cornstarch
2 tablespoons sugar	2 tablespoons sugar
600 ml/1 pint milk (made up with dried milk powder)	2½ cups milk (made up with dried milk powder)
150 ml/¼ pint double cream	⅔ cup heavy cream
4 glacé cherries to decorate	4 glacé cherries to decorate

Make up the jelly (gelatin) following the directions on the packet. When it is on the point of setting, slice two of the bananas and stir them into the jelly. Pour into a glass dish.

When the jelly (gelatin) has cooled but not set, cut the Swiss (jelly) roll into eight and arrange the slices upright around the edge of the dish so that the slices are standing up in the jelly (gelatin).

Blend the cocoa, cornflour (cornstarch) and sugar with a little of the milk Heat the remaining milk then pour it onto the cocoa mixture. Return the sauce to the pan and boil for a couple of minutes, stirring continuously. Cool the sauce.

Lightly whip the cream and fold it into the cold custard. Pour into the dish on top of the jelly (gelatin).

Just before serving, decorate the trifle with slices of the remaining banana and halved glacé cherries.
Serves 6 to 8

Snowy Pudding

METRIC/IMPERIAL	AMERICAN
4 tablespoons pudding rice	4 tablespoons short grain rice
50 g/2 oz dried milk powder, made up to 600 ml/1 pint with water	⅔ cup dried milk powder, made up to 2½ cups with water
1 egg, separated	1 egg, separated
6 tablespoons caster sugar	6 tablespoons sugar
ground nutmeg	ground nutmeg
a little butter	a little butter
1 × 450 g/1 lb can golden plums, drained and stoned	1 × 1 lb can golden plums, drained and pitted

Place the rice, made up milk, beaten egg yolk and half the sugar into a 900 ml/1½ pint (3¾ cup) ovenproof dish and leave to stand for about 15 minutes to allow the rice grains to swell. Sprinkle the top with a little nutmeg and dot with butter.

Cook in a preheated cool oven (150°C/300°F, Gas Mark 2) for about 2 hours.

Take the pudding out of the oven and arrange the drained plums on top.

Whisk the egg white stiffly, add the remaining sugar and whisk again until stiff. Pipe or fork the meringue over the top, allowing the fruit to show through. Cook in a preheated moderate oven (180°C/350°F, Gas Mark 4) for about 15 minutes until the meringue is golden brown.
Cooking time: 2¼ hours
Serves 6

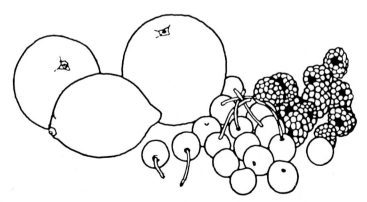

Apple Crisp

METRIC/IMPERIAL	AMERICAN
750 g/1½ lb cooking apples	1½ lb apples
1 teaspoon mixed spice	1 teaspoon apple pie spice
50 g/2 oz butter	¼ cup butter
50 g/2 oz brown sugar	⅓ cup brown sugar
50 g/2 oz cornflakes	2 cups cornflakes
2 tablespoons custard powder	2 tablespoons Bird's English Dessert Mix
2 tablespoons caster sugar	2 tablespoons sugar
600 ml/1 pint milk	2½ cups milk

Peel, core and slice the apples. Cook them with the spice and just enough water to cover the bottom of the pan until the fruit is soft.

Melt the butter in a pan and stir in the brown sugar and cornflakes. Make custard (Dessert Mix) in the usual way using sugar and milk.

Place three-quarters of the cornflake mixture in the bottom of a serving dish. Pour over half the custard, then add a thick layer of apple. Pour on remaining custard and top with the rest of the cornflake mixture.
Cooking time: 30 minutes
Serves 4 to 6

Children's Favourite

METRIC/IMPERIAL	AMERICAN
½ packet orange jelly	½ package orange-flavored gelatin
300 ml/½ pint boiling water	1¼ cups boiling water
1 tablespoon cocoa powder	1 tablespoon unsweetened cocoa
2 tablespoons cornflour	2 tablespoons cornstarch
1 tablespoon sugar	1 tablespoon sugar
300 ml/½ pint milk	1¼ cups milk

Dissolve the jelly (gelatin) in the water. Blend the cocoa, cornflour (cornstarch) and sugar with a little of the milk. Heat the remaining milk in a pan, then pour onto the cocoa and return to the pan. Bring to the boil, stirring continuously. Remove from the heat and gradually blend in the jelly (gelatin).

Pour the mixture into a rinsed 900 ml/1½ pint (3¾ cup) rabbit mould or other fancy mould and leave until set. Turn out just before serving.
Serves 4

Refrigerated Chocolate Fudge Cake

METRIC/IMPERIAL	AMERICAN
225 g/8 oz plain chocolate	8 squares (1 oz each) semi-sweet chocolate
450 g/1 lb digestive biscuits, crushed	6 cups graham cracker crumbs
75 g/3 oz caster sugar	⅓ cup sugar
50 g/2 oz glacé cherries	¼ cup glacé cherries
50 g/2 oz walnuts	½ cup walnuts
1 teaspoon instant coffee powder	1 teaspoon instant coffee powder
50 g/2 oz butter	¼ cup butter
1 × 215 g/7½ oz can evaporated milk	1 × 7½ oz can evaporated milk
2 eggs, beaten	2 eggs, beaten

Line a 1 kg/2 lb (9 × 5 × 3 inch) loaf pan with foil. Break up the chocolate, place in a basin over a pan of hot water and leave until melted.

Place the crumbs in a bowl with the sugar. Chop the cherries and walnuts. Add these with the coffee powder to the biscuit crumb mixture.

Place the butter and evaporated milk in a saucepan. Heat slowly until the butter melts. Mix with the melted chocolate and gradually stir in the eggs.

Pour onto the crumb mixture and stir until thoroughly mixed.

Transfer to the prepared pan and smooth the top with a knife. Refrigerate overnight. Turn out and cut into slices.
Cooking time: 15 minutes
Serves 6 to 8

Orange Charlotte

METRIC/IMPERIAL	AMERICAN
1 tablespoon powdered gelatine	1 tablespoon unflavored gelatin
grated rind and juice of 1 large orange	grated rind and juice of 1 large orange
300 ml/½ pint milk	1¼ cups milk
2 eggs, separated	2 eggs, separated
50 g/2 oz caster sugar	¼ cup sugar
15-16 sponge fingers	15-16 lady finger biscuits
To decorate:	**To decorate:**
whipped cream	whipped cream
a few orange and lemon jelly slices	a few orange and lemon slice candies

Sprinkle the gelatine over the orange juice and leave to soak. Heat the milk and grated orange rind to boiling point. Beat the egg yolks and sugar together in a heatproof bowl until light. Pour on the milk, stir well and place the bowl over a pan of boiling water. Cook, stirring occasionally, until the custard thickens slightly. Stir in the gelatine until dissolved.

Line the base of a 15 cm/6 inch cake tin (pan) or soufflé dish with a circle of greaseproof (waxed) paper. Stand the sponge (lady) fingers upright around the inside of the dish, trimming them to fit neatly.

When the gelatine mixture is just on the point of setting, whisk the egg whites until very stiff and fold into the mixture. Spoon into the dish and leave until firmly set.

Trim the sponge (lady) fingers level with the filling. Run a knife carefully around the inside of the dish, then unmould onto a plate. Peel off the paper.

Decorate with whipped cream and the orange and lemon slices.
Serves 6

Mocha Nut Dessert

METRIC/IMPERIAL	AMERICAN
25 g/1 oz butter	2 tablespoons butter
1 tablespoon golden syrup	1 tablespoon corn syrup
40 g/1½ oz Rice Krispies	1½ cups Rice Krispies
Filling:	**Filling:**
40 g/1½ oz cornflour	6 tablespoons cornstarch
3 teaspoons instant coffee powder	3 teaspoons instant coffee powder
450 ml/¾ pint milk	2 cups milk
150 ml/¼ pint chocolate yogurt	⅔ cup chocolate yogurt
1½ tablespoons hazelnuts, skinned and roughly chopped	1½ tablespoons hazelnuts, skinned and roughly chopped
Topping:	**Topping:**
150 ml/¼ pint hazelnut yogurt	⅔ cup hazelnut yogurt
5 tablespoons double cream, whipped	⅓ cup heavy cream, whipped
To decorate:	**To decorate:**
grated chocolate	grated chocolate
8 whole hazelnuts	8 whole hazelnuts

Melt the butter and syrup together in a pan. Add the Rice Krispies and mix well until coated. Press into the base of an 18cm/7 inch fluted flan (pie) ring on a serving plate. Leave to cool.

Mix the cornflour (cornstarch) and coffee powder with a little of the milk. Heat the remaining milk until boiling and pour onto the cornflour mixture, stirring. Return to the pan and bring back to the boil. Simmer for a few minutes. Remove from the heat, stir in the chocolate yogurt and chopped hazelnuts and pour onto the crispy base.

Mix the hazelnut yogurt with the whipped cream and spread it over the chocolate mixture. Leave in the refrigerator to chill and set.

Carefully remove flan (pie) ring and decorate with grated chocolate and whole hazelnuts. If liked, serve with a chocolate sauce.
Serves 6 to 8

Mocha Nut Dessert
(Photograph: National Dairy Council)

Peach and Cherry Trifle

METRIC/IMPERIAL	AMERICAN
225 g/8 oz black cherries	½ lb bing cherries
3 peaches	3 peaches
150 g/5 oz sugar	⅔ cup sugar
200 ml/⅓ pint water	⅞ cup water
6 individual sponge cakes	6 individual sponge cakes
redcurrant jam	red currant jam
Topping:	**Topping:**
2 tablespoons custard powder	2 tablespoons Bird's English Dessert Mix
450 ml/¾ pint milk	2 cups milk
1½ tablespoons caster sugar	1½ tablespoons sugar
To decorate:	**To decorate:**
50 g/2 oz flaked almonds	½ cup sliced almonds
150 ml/¼ pint double cream	⅔ cup heavy cream

Wash the cherries and peaches and remove the stones (pits). Reserve a few cherries for decoration. Slice two of the peaches. Mix together the cherries and sliced peaches.

Place the sugar and water in a pan and heat gently, stirring, until sugar has dissolved. Bring to the boil, then simmer for 5 minutes. Leave the syrup to cool, then pour it over the fruit.

Split the sponge cakes and spread them with redcurrant jam. Arrange them in the bottom of a serving bowl.

Pour the syrup and fruit over the sponge and leave to soak for 30 minutes. Make up the custard (Dessert Mix) as usual with the milk and sugar and pour over the fruit. Leave to set.

Reserve a few almonds and sprinkle the rest over the custard. Whip the cream until slightly stiff and spread over the trifle.

Slice the remaining peach and arrange with the reserved cherries and almonds on top.
Serves 4 to 6

Fresh Fruit Jelly

METRIC/IMPERIAL	AMERICAN
1½ tablespoons powdered gelatine	1½ tablespoons unflavored gelatin
300 ml/½ pint water	1¼ cups water
2 tablespoons sugar	2 tablespoons sugar
grated rind and juice of 4 oranges	grated rind and juice of 4 oranges
juice of 1 lemon	juice of 1 lemon

Sprinkle the gelatine over a little of the water in a bowl and leave to soak for 5 minutes. Place the bowl over a pan of simmering water and stir to dissolve the gelatine. Add the sugar and stir until dissolved. Leave to cool.

Add the orange rind to the gelatine and leave to stand for 10 minutes. Strain the fruit juices into a jug and stir in the gelatine and remaining water. Pour into a 900 ml/1½ pint (3¾ cup) mould and chill until set.

Unmould onto a serving plate, decorate with fresh fruit and serve with whipped cream.
Serves 4

Coffee Bavarois

METRIC/IMPERIAL	AMERICAN
3 eggs	3 eggs
2 teaspoons cornflour	2 teaspoons cornstarch
2 tablespoons caster sugar	2 tablespoons sugar
2-3 drops vanilla essence	2-3 drops vanilla
450 ml/¾ pint milk	2 cups milk
1 tablespoon instant coffee	1 tablespoon instant coffee
4 teaspoons powdered gelatine	4 teaspoons unflavored gelatin
3 tablespoons hot water	3 tablespoons hot water
150 ml/¼ pint double cream	⅔ cup heavy cream

Cream the eggs with the cornflour (cornstarch) and sugar in a bowl. Add the vanilla essence.

Heat the milk in a pan to just below boiling point and stir in the coffee. Pour onto the egg mixture, blend well and return to the heat. Stir continually until the custard coats the back of a spoon. Strain the custard into a bowl to cool.

Place the gelatine in a small bowl with the hot water and stir until it has dissolved. Leave to cool.

Whip the cream until just thick and fold into the cold custard. Pour in the gelatine in a steady stream, whisking all the time.

Turn the custard into a 900 ml/1½ pint (3¾ cup) mould and leave to set. Unmould carefully onto a serving dish.
Cooking time: 15 minutes
Serves 6

Sunday Special

METRIC/IMPERIAL	AMERICAN
100 g/4 oz butter	½ cup butter
50 g/2 oz caster sugar	¼ cup sugar
200 g/7 oz plain flour, sifted	1¾ cups all-purpose flour, sifted
1 packet raspberry jelly	1 package raspberry-flavored gelatin
150 ml/¼ pint soured cream	⅔ cup sour cream
grated rind and juice of 1 orange	grated rind and juice of 1 orange
450 g/1 lb fresh or frozen and thawed raspberries	1 lb fresh or frozen and thawed raspberries

Cream together the butter and sugar. Mix in the flour and knead lightly to give a soft pastry. Press pastry into the bottom and up the sides of a 20 cm/8 inch flan tin (pie pan). Place pan on a baking tray. Prick the base and cook in a preheated moderate oven (180°C/350°F, Gas Mark 4) for about 30 minutes until golden brown. Allow to cool then remove from the tin.

Dissolve the jelly (gelatin) in a little hot water and make up to 450 ml/¾ pint (2 cups) with cold water. Place 150 ml/¼ pint (⅔ cup) of the cooled jelly (gelatin) in a bowl and stir in the sour cream and orange rind.

When almost set, pour into the flan (pie) case, allow to set and then cover with the raspberries. Add the orange juice to the remaining jelly (gelatin) and, when it is on the point of setting, spoon it over the raspberries to make a glaze. When set, cut into slices to serve.
Cooking time: 30 minutes
Serves 6 to 8

Strawberry Mousse

METRIC/IMPERIAL	AMERICAN
350 g/12 oz fresh strawberries	¾ lb fresh strawberries
100 g/4 oz sugar	½ cup sugar
150 ml/¼ pint red wine or water	⅔ cup red wine or water
1 tablespoon powdered gelatine	1 tablespoon unflavored gelatin
1 egg white	1 egg white
7 tablespoons double cream	7 tablespoons heavy cream
To decorate:	**To decorate:**
whipped cream	whipped cream
a few fresh strawberries	a few fresh strawberries

Place the strawberries and 6 tablespoons of the sugar in a blender or food processor. Heat the red wine or water to just below boiling point. Remove from the heat and sprinkle the gelatine over the surface, whisking briskly with a fork to dissolve. Mix with the blended fruit purée and leave until beginning to thicken.

Whisk the egg white stiffly, then whisk in the remaining sugar to form soft peaks. Whip the cream until it holds its shape and fold into the fruit. Fold in the whisked egg white.

Spoon the mousse into tall glasses and leave to set.

Decorate with whipped cream and whole fresh strawberries.
Serves 4

Fruit Dreams

METRIC/IMPERIAL	AMERICAN
1 orange	1 orange
450 g/1 lb rhubarb, chopped	1 lb rhubarb, chopped
1 tablespoon water	1 tablespoon water
few drops liquid artificial sweetener	few drops liquid artificial sweetener
few drops pink food colouring	few drops pink food coloring
150 ml/¼ pint plain low fat yogurt	⅔ cup plain low fat yogurt
1 large egg white, whisked until stiff	1 large egg white, whisked until stiff
Topping:	**Topping:**
1 tablespoon low calorie spread	1 tablespoon low calorie margarine
25 g/1 oz low calorie fresh breadcrumbs	½ cup low calorie soft bread crumbs
¼ teaspoon mixed spice	¼ teaspoon mixed spice
orange slices to decorate	orange slices to decorate

Grate the rind from the orange and reserve. Remove the white pith, cut the orange into segments and chop them.

Place the rhubarb, water and orange rind in a pan and simmer gently until the rhubarb is tender. Stir in the liquid sweetener to taste. Leave to cool then rub the mixture through a sieve or purée in a blender or food processor.

Mix in a few drops of colouring, the yogurt and chopped orange and fold in the egg white.

Melt the spread (margarine) in a pan and fry the breadcrumbs with the spice for 1 to 2 minutes until browned. Leave to cool.

Layer the rhubarb and breadcrumb mixture into four glasses. Decorate with the orange slices. Serve within 1 hour of making.
Cooking time: 20 minutes
Serves 4
Note: a good recipe if you are watching your weight as it only contains about 70 calories per portion.

Gooseberry and Rice Mousse

METRIC/IMPERIAL	AMERICAN
1 × 450 g/1 lb can creamed rice	1 × 1 lb can creamed rice
450 g/1 lb gooseberries, topped and tailed	1 lb gooseberries, ends removed
4 tablespoons water	4 tablespoons water
100 g/4 oz sugar, or to taste	½ cup sugar, or to taste
½ teaspoon grated orange rind	½ teaspoon grated orange rind
2 teaspoons powdered gelatine	2 teaspoons unflavored gelatin
2 tablespoons orange juice	2 tablespoons orange juice
2 egg whites	2 egg whites
To decorate:	**To decorate:**
a little whipped cream	a little whipped cream
3 orange slices	3 orange slices

Use the rice as it is or rub through a sieve or work in a blender or food processor until it is smooth.

Reserve six gooseberries for decoration and cook the remainder with the water until tender. Add the sugar and leave to cool slightly.

Rub the gooseberries through a sieve or work in a blender or food processor to obtain a smooth purée. Cool completely. Stir the orange rind into the fruit purée then fold in the rice.

Dissolve the gelatine in the orange juice in a small bowl over a pan of hot water. Leave to cool then stir into the mousse. Beat the egg whites stiffly and fold into the mousse. Pour into a bowl or glasses and chill until set.

Decorate with swirls of whipped cream, slices of orange and the reserved gooseberries. Serve with sponge (lady) fingers.
Serves 4 to 6

Gooseberry and Rice Mousse
(Photograph: Ambrosia Milk Puddings)

Blackcurrant Cups

METRIC/IMPERIAL	AMERICAN
1 × 425 g/15 oz can blackcurrants	1 × 15 oz can blackcurrants
2 tablespoons sweet sherry	2 tablespoons sweet sherry
1 packet blackcurrant jelly	1 package blackcurrant-flavored gelatin
500 ml/18 fl oz ice cream	2¼ cups ice cream

Drain the syrup from the blackcurrants and place them in a bowl with the sherry.

Make up the syrup to 300 ml/½ pint (1¼ cups) with water and pour into a pan. Heat the syrup and dissolve the jelly (gelatin) in it. Leave to cool.

Cut the ice cream into rough pieces and whisk into the jelly.

Divide the blackcurrants between six glasses, reserving a few for decoration.

Fill up each glass with the jelly and ice cream mixture and leave to set. Decorate with the remaining blackcurrants before serving.
Serves 6

Chocolate Vanilla Surprise

METRIC/IMPERIAL	AMERICAN
2 tablespoons powdered gelatine	2 tablespoons unflavored gelatin
120 ml/4 fl oz hot water	½ cup hot water
100 g/4 oz sugar	½ cup sugar
750 ml/1¼ pints evaporated milk	3 cups evaporated milk
300 ml/½ pint double cream	1¼ cups heavy cream
2 teaspoons vanilla essence	2 teaspoons vanilla
Chocolate sauce:	**Chocolate sauce:**
225 g/8 oz sugar	1 cup sugar
4 tablespoons cocoa powder	4 tablespoons unsweetened cocoa
120 ml/4 fl oz water	½ cup water

Sprinkle the gelatine over the hot water and stir briskly with a fork until dissolved. Add the sugar and stir until dissolved. Add 4 tablespoons evaporated milk to the gelatine mixture, stirring well. Stir this mixture into the remaining evaporated milk.

Whip the cream until thick. Fold into the milk mixture with the vanilla. Pour into a 1.75 litre/3 pint (2 quart) mould or bowl and refrigerate until firm.

Mix together the sugar, cocoa and water. Place in a pan and boil the mixture for 5 minutes. Leave to cool.

Unmould the vanilla mixture on a serving plate and pour over the chocolate sauce.
Serves 6

Danish Coffee Mousse

METRIC/IMPERIAL	AMERICAN
100 g /4 oz unsalted butter	½ cup unsalted butter
150 ml/¼ pint milk	⅔ cup milk
1 teaspoon powdered gelatine	1 teaspoon unflavored gelatin
1 tablespoon hot water	1 tablespoon hot water
2 eggs, separated	2 eggs, separated
50 g/2 oz caster sugar	¼ cup sugar
2 teaspoons coffee essence	2 teaspoons strong black coffee

Cut the butter into pieces. Place the milk and butter in a pan over a very low heat and melt slowly, stirring from time to time. Pour the lukewarm milk mixture into a blender and mix at maximum speed for 30 seconds. Cover and chill for 1-2 hours then whip this cream until stiff.

Place the gelatine in a small bowl with the hot water and stir until dissolved.

Place the egg yolks in a bowl with the sugar and whisk over a pan of hot water until light and fluffy. Stir in the coffee and dissolved gelatine.

Whisk the egg whites until stiff and carefully fold into the coffee mixture. Fold in two-thirds of the whipped cream. Pour into a serving dish or individual glasses and chill until set. Use the remaining cream to decorate the mousse.
Serves 4

Pear Condé

METRIC/IMPERIAL	AMERICAN
3 tablespoons pudding rice	3 tablespoons short grain rice
2 tablespoons caster sugar	2 tablespoons sugar
600 ml/1 pint milk (made up with dried milk powder)	2½ cups milk (made up with dried milk powder)
1 × 225 g/8 oz can pear halves	1 × 8 oz can pear halves
1 teaspoon arrowroot	1 teaspoon arrowroot
red food colouring	red food coloring
8 angelica diamonds to decorate	8 angelica diamonds to decorate

Place rice, sugar and milk in a heavy-based pan and cook gently for 30 to 35 minutes, stirring occasionally, until thick and creamy. Leave to cool. Divide between four sundae glasses. Drain the pears and reserve the juice. Place a pear half in each dish, cut side down. In a small saucepan, mix the arrowroot with a little pear juice and blend in the rest. Gently bring the glaze to the boil, stirring continuously, until thickened. Add a few drops of red food colouring. Allow to cool, then spoon over the pear halves.

Place two angelica diamonds on each pear.
Cooking time: 40 minutes
Serves 4

Pineapple and Yogurt Cheesecake

METRIC/IMPERIAL	AMERICAN
5 digestive biscuits	5 graham crackers
1 × 225 g/8 oz can pineapple rings in natural juice	1 × 8 oz can pineapple rings in natural juice
½ packet lemon jelly	½ package lemon-flavored gelatin
225 g/8 oz cottage cheese, sieved	1 cup cottage cheese, strained
150 ml/¼ pint plain low fat yogurt	⅔ cup plain low fat yogurt

Arrange the biscuits (crackers) in an 18 cm/7 inch flan (pie) ring on a plate.

Drain the pineapple and reserve the juice. Reserve two pineapple rings and chop the remainder. Make up the juice to 150 ml/¼ pint (⅔ cup) with water. Pour into a pan and add the jelly (gelatin). Stir over a low heat until the jelly (gelatin) has dissolved. Leave on one side to cool but not set.

Mix together the cheese, chopped pineapple and yogurt. Stir in the cool jelly and chill until beginning to set.

Spread the mixture over the biscuits (crackers) and leave to set completely. Remove flan (pie) ring. Decorate with pineapple.
Serves 6

Queen of Puddings

METRIC/IMPERIAL	AMERICAN
2 low calorie rolls, crumbed	2 low calorie rolls, crumbed
2 eggs, separated	2 eggs, separated
300 ml/½ pint skimmed milk	1¼ cups skimmed milk
artificial sweetener to taste	artificial sweetener to taste
4 teaspoons low calorie strawberry jam	4 teaspoons low calorie strawberry jam

Place the crumbs in an ovenproof dish. Beat the egg yolks and skimmed milk together and pour over the breadcrumbs.

Cook in a preheated moderate oven (180°C/350°F, Gas Mark 4) for 45 minutes until firm. Remove from the oven and then increase the oven temperature to moderately hot (200°C/400°F, Gas Mark 6).

Whisk the egg whites until stiff and fold in the sweetener. Spread the jam over the custard mixture. Pipe or spread the egg white on top. Cook for 10 minutes until lightly brown.
Cooking time: 55 minutes
Serves 4
Note: a tempting recipe for all the family and it has only 43 calories per portion.

Pastry Desserts

Apple Strudel

METRIC/IMPERIAL	AMERICAN
275 g/10 oz plain flour	2½ cups all-purpose flour
pinch of salt	pinch of salt
1 teaspoon butter or margarine	1 teaspoon butter or margarine
1 egg	1 egg
150 ml/¼ pint lukewarm water	⅔ cup lukewarm water
1 egg yolk to glaze	1 egg yolk to glaze
150 ml/¼ pint soured cream	⅔ cup sour cream
Filling:	**Filling:**
75 g/3 oz butter, melted	6 tablespoons butter, melted
50 g/2 oz fresh breadcrumbs	1 cup soft bread crumbs
1.5 kg/3 lb apples, peeled, cored and sliced	3 lb apples, peeled, cored and sliced
50 g/2 oz raisins	⅓ cup raisins
75 g/3 oz caster sugar	⅓ cup sugar
½ teaspoon ground cinnamon	½ teaspoon ground cinnamon

Sift the flour and salt into a bowl. Add the fat, egg and water and knead well. Form into a round loaf shape, place in a warm bowl and leave covered for 20 minutes.

Place a clean tea-towel (dish cloth) on a working surface and sprinkle with flour. Roll out the pastry very thinly on the cloth. Flour your hands and place them under the dough and pull very gently and evenly until it is paper thin. Trim edges and brush the dough with the melted butter.

Sprinkle the breadcrumbs over the dough. Mix together the apples, raisins, sugar and cinnamon and place on the dough. Roll up dough and seal edges with water. Place roll on a greased baking sheet, curving the ends of the strudel to make a horseshoe shape.

Beat the egg yolk and then brush it over the strudel. Cook in a preheated hot oven (220°C/425°F, Gas Mark 7) for 30 minutes until golden brown. Spoon over the soured cream and continue cooking for another 10 minutes.

Serve hot or cold, sprinkled with sugar.
Cooking time: 40 minutes
Serves 6

Apricot Choux Ring

METRIC/IMPERIAL	AMERICAN
50 g/2 oz butter	¼ cup butter
150 ml/¼ pint water	¾ cup water
65 g/2½ oz plain flour	¾ cup all-purpose flour
2 eggs	2 eggs
Filling:	**Filling:**
50 g/2 oz browned hazelnuts	⅓ cup browned hazelnuts
300 ml/½ pint double cream, whipped	1¼ cups heavy cream, whipped
350 g/12 oz fresh apricots, halved and stoned	¾ lb fresh apricots, halved and pitted

Melt the butter in the water in a pan, bring to the boil and remove from the heat immediately. Add the flour all at once and beat with a wooden spoon until the mixture leaves the sides of the pan and forms a soft ball. Cool slightly, then beat in the eggs, one at a time, until the mixture is smooth and shiny.

Place mixture in a piping (pastry) bag fitted with a 1.5 cm/¾ inch plain nozzle and pipe a 20 cm/8 inch ring onto a greased baking tray.

Cook in a preheated moderately hot oven (200°C/400°F, Gas Mark 6) for 20 to 30 minutes until risen and golden. Make some slits on the inner edge to allow steam to escape and return to the oven for 5 to 10 minutes to dry out. Leave to cool on a wire rack.

Chop half of the nuts. Whip the cream until stiff and fold in half of the apricots and the chopped nuts. Split the choux ring in half horizontally. Fill with the apricot cream mixture and place on a serving plate. Fill the centre of the ring with the remaining apricots and nuts.
Cooking time: 45 minutes
Serves 6

Apple Strudel
(Photograph: Hungarian Wines)

Toffee Apple Flan

METRIC/IMPERIAL	AMERICAN
Pastry:	**Dough:**
200 g/7 oz plain flour	1¾ cups all-purpose
pinch of salt	flour
150 g/5 oz butter	pinch of salt
2 teaspoons caster	½ cup + 2
sugar	tablespoons butter
1 egg, beaten	2 teaspoons sugar
about 2 tablespoons	1 egg, beaten
cold water	about 2 tablespoons
Almond cream:	cold water
4 egg yolks	**Almond cream:**
100 g/4 oz sugar	4 egg yolks
50 g/2 oz plain flour	½ cup caster sugar
450 ml/¾ pint milk	½ cup all-purpose
50 g/2 oz ground	flour
almonds	2 cups milk
few drops vanilla	½ cup ground
essence	almonds
few drops almond	few drops vanilla
essence	few drops almond
Topping:	extract
2 green dessert	**Topping:**
apples	2 green-skinned
2 red dessert apples	apples
15 g/½ oz butter,	2 red-skinned apples
melted	1 tablespoon melted
225 g/8 oz granulated	butter
sugar	1 cup sugar

First make the pastry: sieve the flour and salt into a bowl, rub (cut) in the butter and stir in the sugar. Add the egg and sufficient cold water to bind to a pliable dough. Roll out and line a flan dish (pie pan) and bake blind (unfilled) in a preheated moderately hot oven (190°C/375°F, Gas Mark 5) for 15 minutes.

Beat the egg yolks and sugar together until thick and creamy. Stir in the flour. Heat the milk in a pan until almost boiling then pour the milk onto the egg mixture, stirring continuously. Return to the pan and bring to the boil, stirring, until the mixture thickens. Remove from the heat, stir in the ground almonds and vanilla and almond essences (extracts). Allow to cool then pour into the flan.

Quarter apples, remove cores and cut into slices. Arrange apple slices over almond filling. Brush with butter and cook in a preheated moderately hot oven (190°C/375°F, Gas Mark 5) for 10 minutes. Remove from the oven.

Melt the sugar in a heavy-based pan until golden and pour over the apples. Serve hot.
Cooking time: 35 minutes
Serves 8

Blackberry and Apple Shortbread

METRIC/IMPERIAL	AMERICAN
50 g/2 oz butter	¼ cup butter
75 g/3 oz plain flour	¾ cup all-purpose
2 tablespoons caster	flour
sugar	2 tablespoons sugar
50 g/2 oz flaked	½ cup sliced
almonds, toasted	almonds, toasted
1 × 400 g/14 oz can	1 × 14 oz can
blackberry and	blackberry and
apple pie filling	apple pie filling

Knead the butter, flour, sugar and half the almonds together to make a stiff dough. Press into an 18 cm/7 inch round on a greased baking sheet. Crimp up the edge so that the shortbread will hold the filling.

Cook in a preheated moderately hot oven (190°C/375°F, Gas Mark 5) for 10 to 15 minutes. Allow to cool a little, then place on a plate and leave to cool completely. Arrange pie filling on shortbread. Sprinkle over remaining almonds.
Cooking time: 15 minutes
Serves 4

Flaky Mandarin Whirls

METRIC/IMPERIAL	AMERICAN
75 g/3 oz dried figs	½ cup dried figs
400 g/14 oz frozen	14 oz frozen puff
puff pastry, thawed	pastry, thawed
1 × 450 g/16 oz can	1 × 16 oz can
mandarin orange	mandarin orange
segments, drained	segments, drained
225 g/8 oz mixed	1⅓ cups chopped
chopped peel	mixed candied peel
¼ teaspoon grated	¼ teaspoon grated
nutmeg	nutmeg
2 tablespoons caster	2 tablespoons sugar
sugar	

Soak the figs in water for 3 hours, then drain and chop them. Roll out the pastry to form a large rectangle 35 × 40 cm/14 × 16 inches.

Sprinkle oranges, mixed peel, figs, nutmeg and half the sugar over the pastry. Starting at one shorter side, roll up tightly. Trim the ends then cut the roll into six equal rounds. Place rounds, cut-side down, in a flan tin (pie pan). Sprinkle over remaining sugar.

Cook in a preheated hot oven (220°C/425°F, Gas Mark 7) for 35 to 40 minutes.
Cooking time: 35 to 40 minutes
Serves 6

Hazy Day Flan

METRIC/IMPERIAL	AMERICAN
65 g/2½ oz butter	5 tablespoons butter
2 tablespoons caster sugar	2 tablespoons sugar
150 g/5 oz plain flour	1¼ cups all-purpose flour
1 egg yolk	1 egg yolk
1 tablespoon cold water	1 tablespoon cold water
Filling:	**Filling:**
150 ml/¼ pint milk	⅔ cup milk
1 teaspoon ground cinnamon	1 teaspoon ground cinnamon
grated rind of 1 lemon	grated rind of 1 lemon
2 large eggs	2 large eggs
To decorate:	**To decorate:**
225 g/8 oz fresh strawberries	½ lb fresh strawberries
150 ml/¼ pint double cream, lightly whipped	⅔ cup heavy cream, lightly whipped

Place the butter, sugar and flour in a bowl and rub (cut) in the butter. Knead to a smooth dough with the egg yolk and water. Roll out and line an 18 cm/7 inch flan tin (pie pan).

Beat together the milk, cinnamon, lemon rind and eggs. Pour into the flan (pie) case. Cook in a preheated moderately hot oven (190°C/375°F, Gas Mark 5) for 30 to 35 minutes. Leave to cool.

Decorate with strawberries and cream.
Cooking time: 30 to 35 minutes
Serves 4 to 6

Gooseberry Tartlets

METRIC/IMPERIAL	AMERICAN
75 g/3 oz butter	6 tablespoons butter
175 g/6 oz plain flour	1½ cups all-purpose flour
2 tablespoons caster sugar	2 tablespoons sugar
1 egg yolk	1 egg yolk
1 tablespoon water	1 tablespoon water
Filling:	**Filling:**
350 g/12 oz fresh gooseberries	¾ lb fresh gooseberries
a little water	a little water
50 g/2 oz sugar	¼ cup sugar
150 ml/¼ pint double cream	⅔ cup heavy cream

Place the butter and flour in a bowl and rub (cut) in the butter until the mixture resembles fine breadcrumbs. Stir in the sugar. Beat together the egg yolk and water and stir in to form a stiff dough. Knead lightly and chill for 30 minutes.

Roll out the pastry and, using a 7.5 cm/3 inch fluted cutter, cut out 12 to 16 rounds. Press into patty tins (pans) and prick the bottom of each with a fork.

Cook in a preheated moderately hot oven (200°C/400°F, Gas Mark 6) for 10 to 15 minutes until golden brown.

Cook the gooseberries in a few tablespoons of water with the sugar until soft. Reserve some whole gooseberries for decoration and purée the remainder. Leave to cool.

Whisk the cream until thick and fold into the cooled gooseberry purée. Adjust sweetening to taste and spoon into pastry cases.

Decorate with reserved gooseberries.
Cooking time: 30 minutes
Makes 12 to 16 tartlets

Honey Plum Cobbler

METRIC/IMPERIAL	AMERICAN
1 kg/2 lb ripe plums, halved and stoned	2 lb ripe plums, halved and pitted
4-6 tablespoons clear honey	4-6 tablespoons honey
225 g/8 oz self-raising flour	2 cups self-rising flour
2 tablespoons sugar	2 tablespoons sugar
50 g/2 oz butter or margarine	¼ cup butter or margarine
1 egg, beaten	1 egg, beaten
5-6 tablespoons milk	5-6 tablespoons milk

Place the plums in an ovenproof dish with the honey and cover with foil. Cook in a preheated moderately hot oven (200°C/400°F, Gas Mark 6) for 15 minutes.

Meanwhile mix together the flour and sugar and rub in the fat. Using a knife, gradually stir in the egg and milk to form a fairly soft dough. Roll out on a floured surface to about 1.5 cm/¾ inch thick and cut out rounds using a 5 cm/2 inch cutter. Remove the plums from the oven, cool slightly and arrange the rounds in an overlapping circle on top of the plums. Brush with milk and sprinkle with a little sugar. Cook for about 30 minutes or until golden brown.

Serve piping hot with fresh cream.
Cooking time: 45 minutes
Serves 4 to 6

Chocolate Meringue Pie

METRIC/IMPERIAL	AMERICAN
75 g/3 oz butter	6 tablespoons butter
175 g/6 oz plain flour	1½ cups all-purpose
25 g/1 oz icing sugar	flour
1 egg yolk	¼ cup confectioners
Filling and topping:	sugar
175 ml/6 fl oz	1 egg yolk
evaporated milk	**Filling and topping:**
50 g/2 oz cornflour	¾ cup evaporated
2 tablespoons	milk
chocolate powder	½ cup cornstarch
large pinch ground	2 tablespoons
cinnamon	sweetened cocoa
2 eggs, separated	large pinch ground
100 g/4 oz caster	cinnamon
sugar	2 eggs, separated
	½ cup sugar

Rub (cut) the butter into the flour. Add the sugar, egg yolk and just enough water to bind the dough together. Roll out the pastry on a lightly floured surface and carefully line an 18 cm/7 inch flan ring (pie pan). Trim the edges and prick the base with a fork. Line with greaseproof (waxed) paper and dried beans and bake in a preheated moderately hot oven (190°C/375°F, Gas Mark 5) for about 25 minutes. Remove the paper and beans for the last 5 minutes and take off the flan (pie) ring.

Make up the evaporated milk to 450 ml/¾ pint (2 cups) with water. Blend the cornflour (cornstarch) in a saucepan with a little evaporated milk and, when smooth, add all the milk, chocolate (cocoa) and cinnamon. Bring to the boil, stirring continuously, until thickened. Cool a little, then stir in the egg yolks. Pour the filling into the pastry case.

Whisk the egg whites until very stiff. Add half the sugar and whisk again until the meringue is stiff. Fold in the remaining sugar and spread on top of the filling.

Brown slightly in a preheated hot oven (220°C/425°F, Gas Mark 7) for no longer than 5 minutes until pale brown. Serve hot or cold.
Cooking time: 40 minutes
Serves 6 to 8

Linzertorte

METRIC/IMPERIAL	AMERICAN
75 g/3 oz plain flour	¾ cup all-purpose
½ teaspoon ground	flour
cinnamon	½ teaspoon ground
75 g/3 oz caster sugar	cinnamon
75 g/3 oz ground	⅓ cup sugar
almonds	¾ cup ground
grated rind of	almonds
½ lemon	grated rind of
100 g/4 oz unsalted	½ lemon
butter	½ cup unsalted butter
2 egg yolks	2 egg yolks
¼ teaspoon vanilla	¼ teaspoon vanilla
essence	¾ lb thick raspberry
350 g/12 oz thick	jam
raspberry jam	**Glaze:**
Glaze:	1 egg yolk
1 egg yolk	1 tablespoon heavy
1 tablespoon double	cream
cream	

Sieve the flour, cinnamon and sugar into a bowl. Add the ground almonds and finely grated lemon rind. Rub (cut) in the butter until the mixture resembles fine breadcrumbs.

Beat together the egg yolks and vanilla and stir into the flour mixture. Mix to a soft dough and wrap and chill for 1 hour.

Grease a 25 cm/10 inch flan (pie) dish. Knead dough lightly. Reserve just under a quarter of the dough for the lattice topping. Press the remaining dough over the base and up the sides of the dish.

Spread the jam evenly over the bottom of the flan (pie). Roll out remaining dough on a well-floured board to form a rectangle 20 × 7.5 cm/8 × 3 inches. Cut into six strips.

Carefully lift the strips and lay them across the jam in a lattice pattern. Run a knife around the top edge of the flan (pie) dish to loosen the pastry and fold it inwards and down onto the jam to make a 1 cm/½ inch wide border.

Beat together the remaining egg yolk and cream and brush over the lattice and border. Chill for 30 minutes.

Cook in the centre of a preheated moderate oven (180°C/350°F, Gas Mark 4) for 35 to 45 minutes, until crisp and lightly browned. Leave to cool then serve with whipped cream.
Cooking time: 35 to 45 minutes
Serves 8

Linzertorte
(Photograph: Corning, the manufacturers of Pyrex Glassware)

Avocado Snaps

METRIC/IMPERIAL	AMERICAN
50 g/2 oz golden syrup	3 tablespoons corn syrup
50 g/2 oz plain flour	½ cup all-purpose flour
pinch of salt	pinch of salt
½ teaspoon ground ginger	½ teaspoon ground ginger
50 g/2 oz softened butter	¼ cup softened butter
50 g/2 oz caster sugar	¼ cup sugar
Sweet avocado cream:	**Sweet avocado cream:**
1 ripe avocado, peeled and stoned	1 ripe avocado, peeled and seeded
1 teaspoon icing sugar	1 teaspoon confectioners sugar
2 tablespoons stiffly whipped double cream	2 tablespoons stiffly whipped heavy cream
1 teaspoon brandy or lime juice	1 teaspoon brandy or lime juice

Place the syrup, flour, salt, ginger, butter and sugar in a bowl. Mix together with a knife and then knead by hand until smooth. Divide into 16 pieces.

Roll each piece into a ball and place them about 13 cm/5 inches apart on lightly greased baking trays. Cook in a preheated moderate oven (160°C/325°F, Gas Mark 3) for about 10 minutes. Roll each ginger snap around the greased handle of a wooden spoon as soon as possible and cool on a wire tray.

To make the avocado cream: beat the avocado flesh with a fork until it is a fairly smooth cream. Beat in the sugar. Fold in the cream and brandy or lime juice.

Pile the cream into a small bowl with the ginger snaps arranged round it. Dip the ginger snaps into the cream. Alternatively, pipe the cream into each end of the ginger snaps and arrange on a serving plate.

Cooking time: 10 minutes
Makes 16

Plum Flan

METRIC/IMPERIAL	AMERICAN
225 g/8 oz plain flour	2 cups all-purpose flour
large pinch of salt	large pinch of salt
75 g/3 oz butter	6 tablespoons butter
75 g/3 oz lard	6 tablespoons lard
150 ml/¼ pint water	⅔ cup water
1 egg, beaten	1 egg, beaten
Filling:	**Filling:**
4 plums	4 plums
3 tablespoons redcurrant jelly	3 tablespoons red currant jelly

Mix together the flour and salt in a bowl. Cut the fats into nut-sized pieces and add to the flour. Using a round-bladed knife, stir in the water and mix to a dough. Leave the dough, covered, in a cool place for 15 minutes.

Roll out the dough to a long strip, 13 × 30 cm/5 × 12 inches. Fold the top third down over the middle third, fold up the bottom third and press edges firmly to seal. Leave covered in a cool place for 15 minutes. Repeat rolling, folding and resting in a cool place twice more.

Roll out the pastry to a rectangle, about 25 × 15 cm/10 × 6 inches. Fold in half lengthwise. Cut out a rectangle from the folded edge, leaving a 2.5 cm/1 inch wide band on the remaining three sides. Open out the small rectangle and roll out until 25 × 15 cm/10 × 6 inches. Place on a dampened baking sheet, prick all over and dampen the edges. Open out the band of pastry and place on the rectangle to make a border. Knock up the edges and mark a criss-cross pattern on the border with a knife.

Brush the border with egg and cook in a preheated hot oven (220°C/425°F, Gas Mark 7) for 25 minutes.

Halve plums and remove stones. Arrange plums in the centre of the flan (pie), skin side up. Melt redcurrant jelly in a pan and pour over the plums. Reduce oven temperature to moderately hot (190°C/375°F, Gas Mark 5) and return to the oven for a further 10 minutes.

Cooking time: 35 minutes
Serves 4

Avocado and Strawberry Mille Feuille

METRIC/IMPERIAL	AMERICAN
1 × 375 g/13 oz packet frozen puff pastry	13 oz package frozen puff pastry
2 ripe avocados, peeled and stoned	2 ripe avocados, peeled and seeded
2 teaspoons icing sugar	2 teaspoons confectioners sugar
4 tablespoons stiffly whipped double cream	4 tablespoons stiffly whipped heavy cream
2 teaspoons lime juice, rum or brandy	2 teaspoons lime juice, rum or brandy
4 tablespoons strawberry jam	4 tablespoons strawberry jam
225 g/8 oz strawberries, halved	½ lb strawberries, halved
Icing:	**Icing:**
100 g/4 oz icing sugar, sifted	1 cup sifted confectioners sugar
1 tablespoon warm water	1 tablespoon warm water
green food colouring (optional)	green food coloring (optional)

Roll out the pastry to form an oblong 28 × 30 cm/11 × 12 inches and trim edges. Cut into two oblongs, each 14 × 30 cm/5½ × 12 inches. Make a criss-cross pattern on the top of one piece using a sharp knife – this will be the top of the mille feuille.

Cook in a preheated hot oven (220°C/425°F, Gas Mark 7) for about 15 minutes until well risen and lightly browned. Cool on a wire tray. Carefully split each piece in half through the middle.

Beat the flesh of the avocados with a fork until a fairly smooth cream. Beat in the sugar. Fold in cream and lime juice, rum or brandy.

Place one piece of pastry on a serving plate. Spread over half the avocado cream. Cover with another piece of pastry, spread with the jam and cover with the strawberries, cut side down. Put on a third piece of pastry and spread with the remaining avocado cream. Top with the scored pastry.

Combine the icing sugar, warm water and green colouring, if using, to make a thin glacé icing. Pour the icing over the top and leave it to trickle over the sides.

Cooking time: 15 minutes
Serves 6 to 8

Apricot and Almond Tart

METRIC/IMPERIAL	AMERICAN
100 g/4 oz plain flour	1 cup all-purpose flour
pinch of salt	pinch of salt
50 g/2 oz butter, softened	¼ cup butter, softened
50 g/2 oz icing sugar	½ cup confectioners sugar
2 egg yolks	2 egg yolks
Filling:	**Filling:**
300 ml/½ pint milk	1¼ cups milk
2 tablespoons caster sugar	2 tablespoons sugar
25 g/1 oz cornflour	¼ cup cornstarch
2 egg yolks	2 egg yolks
¼ teaspoon almond essence	¼ teaspoon almond extract
Topping:	**Topping:**
2 × 275 g/10 oz cans apricot halves in fruit juice	2 × 10 oz cans apricot halves in fruit juice
24 whole almonds, blanched and toasted	24 whole almonds, blanched and toasted
1 teaspoon arrowroot	1 teaspoon arrowroot

Sift the flour and salt into a bowl. Make a well in the centre and add the butter, icing sugar and egg yolks. Work the ingredients together, drawing in the flour from the edges until a soft dough is formed. Roll out on a lightly floured surface and use to line a 20 cm/8 inch flan tin (pie pan). Chill for 30 minutes. Prick the base with a fork then bake blind (unfilled) in a preheated moderately hot oven (190°C/375°F, Gas Mark 5) for 20 to 25 minutes until golden. Leave to cool then remove from tin.

Meanwhile make the filling: heat the milk and sugar in a pan. Mix together the cornflour (cornstarch) and egg yolks then pour on the milk. Stir well and strain back into the pan. Cook over the heat, stirring constantly, until the mixture has thickened.

Remove from the heat and stir in the almond essence (extract). Allow to cool then spread over the bottom of the pastry case.

Drain the apricots, reserving the juice from one can and arrange rounded side down on the custard. Place an almond in each apricot half.

Stir the arrowroot into the apricot juice. Bring to the boil, stirring, until thickened. Allow to cool slightly then brush over the apricots to glaze them.

Cooking time: 20 to 25 minutes
Serves 6

Ice Creams & Ices

Blackberry and Honey Ice Cream

METRIC/IMPERIAL	AMERICAN
225 g/8 oz blackberries	½ lb blackberries
2 tablespoons clear honey	2 tablespoons honey
150 ml/¼ pint water	⅔ cup water
4 tablespoons sugar	4 tablespoons sugar
300 ml/½ pint double cream	1¼ cups heavy cream
150 ml/¼ pint single cream	⅔ cup light cream

Cook the blackberries in a pan with the honey, water and sugar for about 5 minutes. Leave to cool. Rub the fruit mixture through a sieve or purée in a blender or food processor. Chill.

Beat the double (heavy) cream until thick and then stir in the single (light) cream. Fold the cream into the cold fruit mixture.

Pour into a rigid freezerproof container and freeze until almost firm. Remove and beat well, then re-freeze until firm.

Serves 6 to 8

Honey Brown Bread Ice Cream

METRIC/IMPERIAL	AMERICAN
600 ml/1 pint double or whipping cream	2½ cups heavy or whipping cream
4 tablespoons honey	4 tablespoons honey
75 g/3 oz icing sugar	⅔ cup confectioners sugar
100 g/4 oz fresh brown breadcrumbs	2 cups soft brown bread crumbs
2 tablespoons rum (optional)	2 tablespoons rum (optional)
2 egg whites	2 egg whites
wafer biscuits to serve	wafer biscuits to serve

Whisk the cream until stiff. Fold in the honey, sugar, breadcrumbs and rum, if using. Whisk the egg whites until firm and fold them into the mixture.

Pour into a 1.2 litre/2 pint (5 cup) rigid freezerproof container and freeze until firm. Remove from the freezer 10 minutes before serving and scoop into dishes. Serve with fan wafer biscuits.

Serves 6 to 8

Blackberry and Honey Ice Cream; Honey Brown Bread Ice Cream; Frozen Raspberry Fool (page 48) (Photograph: Gales Honey Bureau)

Frozen Raspberry Fool

METRIC/IMPERIAL	AMERICAN
350 g/12 oz fresh or frozen raspberries	¾ lb fresh or frozen raspberries
50 g/2 oz sugar	¼ cup sugar
3 tablespoons clear honey	3 tablespoons honey
300 ml/½ pint double cream	1¼ cups heavy cream
few extra raspberries to decorate	few extra raspberries to decorate

Mix together the raspberries, sugar and honey and purée in a blender or food processor or mash with a fork. Whip the cream and fold into the fruit. Pour into a rigid freezerproof container and freeze until firm.

Remove from the freezer a few minutes before serving and scoop into dishes. Decorate with a few extra raspberries.
Serves 4
Illustrated on page 46

Banana Ice Cream

METRIC/IMPERIAL	AMERICAN
450 g/1 lb bananas	1 lb bananas
150 ml/¼ pint double cream	⅔ cup heavy cream
150 ml/¼ pint plain yogurt	⅔ cup plain yogurt
2 tablespoons lemon juice	2 tablespoons lemon juice
5 tablespoons honey	5 tablespoons honey
50 g/2 oz chopped nuts	½ cup chopped nuts
2 egg whites	2 egg whites

Peel and mash the bananas. Add the cream, yogurt, lemon juice, honey and nuts. Beat well until thoroughly mixed.

Place the mixture in a rigid freezerproof container with a lid and freeze until mushy.

Whisk the egg whites until stiff. Fold them into the banana mixture and freeze until firm. Remove from the freezer and place in the refrigerator for 30 minutes before serving.
Serves 6

Melon Melba

METRIC/IMPERIAL	AMERICAN
1 kg/2 lb watermelon	2 lb watermelon
4 tablespoons kirsch (optional)	4 tablespoons kirsch (optional)
6 large scoops vanilla ice cream	6 large scoops vanilla ice cream
Sauce:	**Sauce:**
1 tablespoon golden syrup	1 tablespoon corn syrup
7 g/¼ oz butter	1 tablespoon butter
2 tablespoons demerara sugar	2 tablespoons brown sugar
300 ml/½ pint warm water	1¼ cups warm water
squeeze of lemon juice	squeeze of lemon juice
2 teaspoons cornflour	2 teaspoons cornstarch

Cut the melon flesh into cubes, discarding the skin and seeds. Divide between six serving dishes. Sprinkle with the kirsch, if using, and chill well.

Place the syrup, butter and sugar in a pan and stir over a gentle heat until the sugar has dissolved. Bring to the boil and continue boiling until it is a rich caramel colour. Remove from the heat and carefully add the water and lemon juice.

Blend the cornflour (cornstarch) with a little cold water. Bring the caramel to the boil again and pour onto the blended cornflour, stirring continuously. Return to the pan and simmer for 2 to 3 minutes. Allow to cool slightly.

Top each dish of watermelon with a scoop of vanilla ice cream and pour over the warm caramel sauce. Serve immediately.
Serves 6

Nesselrode Ice Cream

METRIC/IMPERIAL	AMERICAN
3 egg yolks	3 egg yolks
100 g/4 oz sugar	½ cup sugar
300 ml/½ pint milk	1¼ cups milk
225 g/8 oz unsweetened chestnut purée	1 cup unsweetened chestnut purée
3 tablespoons honey	3 tablespoons honey
300 ml/½ pint double cream, lightly whipped	1¼ cups heavy cream, lightly whipped
2 tablespoons glacé peel	2 tablespoons candied peel
2 tablespoons glacé cherries	2 tablespoons glacé cherries
50 g/2 oz raisins	⅓ cup golden raisins
4 tablespoons Marsala or sweet sherry	4 tablespoons Marsala or sweet sherry

Beat the egg yolks and sugar together. Heat the milk with the chestnut purée and honey, stirring until quite smooth. When nearly boiling, pour the milk mixture over the egg yolks and sugar, stirring well. Place the bowl over a pan of simmering water and stir until thickened. Leave to cool.

Fold in the lightly whipped cream. Pour into a rigid freezerproof container and freeze until the mixture begins to set.

Chop the peel and cherries and soak them with the raisins in the Marsala or sherry. When the cream mixture is half set, fold in the fruit and freeze completely.

Remove from the freezer 10 minutes before serving and scoop into dishes.
Serves 4 to 6

Blackcurrant Sorbet

METRIC/IMPERIAL	AMERICAN
1 kg/2 lb fresh or frozen blackcurrants	2 lb fresh or frozen blackcurrants
225 g/8 oz sugar	1 cup sugar
300 ml/½ pint water	1¼ cups water
2 egg whites	2 egg whites

Place all the ingredients except the egg whites into a saucepan. Heat slowly and cook for about 15 minutes or until the blackcurrants are soft. Stir from time to time.

Rub the fruit mixture through a sieve (strainer) and pour into a rigid freezerproof container with a lid. Place in the freezer until the mixture is mushy.

Whisk the egg whites until firm and fold into the blackcurrant mixture. Return to the freezer until firm. Remove from the freezer a few minutes before serving.
Serves 4 to 6

Watermelon Sorbet

METRIC/IMPERIAL
1.5 kg/3 lb watermelon
300 ml/½ pint water
175 g/6 oz caster sugar
juice of ½ lemon
2 egg whites
2 teaspoons freshly chopped mint
mint leaves to decorate

AMERICAN
3 lb watermelon
1¼ cups water
¾ cup sugar
juice of ½ lemon
2 egg whites
2 teaspoons freshly chopped mint
mint leaves to decorate

Remove the skin and seeds from the melon. Roughly chop the melon and purée it in a blender or food processor to make 900 ml/ 1½ pints (3¾ cups) purée in all.

Place the water and sugar in a pan over a low heat and stir until the sugar has dissolved. Slowly bring to the boil and simmer for 10 minutes; cool. Add the syrup and lemon juice to the melon. Pour into a rigid freezerproof container and freeze for 3 to 4 hours until half frozen. Remove from the freezer.

Whisk the egg whites until very stiff and fold into the frozen mixture with the chopped mint. Return the mixture to the container and re-freeze.

Serve spoonfuls of the sorbet in glass dishes, decorated with mint leaves.
Serves 6 to 8

Strawberry Yogurt Ice

METRIC/IMPERIAL
225 g/8 oz fresh or frozen and thawed strawberries
300 ml/½ pint plain low fat yogurt
2 teaspoons powdered gelatine
2 tablespoons water
1 egg white
65 g/2½ oz caster sugar
a few strawberries to decorate

AMERICAN
½ lb fresh or frozen and thawed strawberries
1¼ cups plain low fat yogurt
2 teaspoons unflavored gelatin
2 tablespoons water
1 egg white
⅓ cup firmly packed sugar
a few strawberries to decorate

Place the strawberries and yogurt in a blender or food processor and blend until smooth.

Sprinkle the gelatine over the water in a small bowl. Place the bowl in a pan of hot water and stir until dissolved. Cool slightly then gradually blend into the strawberry mixture.

Pour into an ice tray or shallow container and freeze until becoming icy around the edges. Transfer the mixture to a bowl and beat until smooth.

Whisk the egg white until stiff. Gradually whisk in the sugar, then fold into the strawberry mixture. Pour back into the container and freeze until just frozen.

Spoon or scoop into glasses and decorate with a few extra strawberries.
Serves 6

*Strawberry Yogurt Ice
(Photograph: National Dairy Council)*

Ogen Alaska

METRIC/IMPERIAL	AMERICAN
3 ripe Ogen melons	3 ripe Ogen melons
4 egg whites	4 egg whites
pinch of salt	pinch of salt
100 g/4 oz caster sugar	½ cup sugar
500 ml/18 fl oz vanilla ice cream	2¼ cups vanilla ice cream
2 tablespoons halved blanched almonds (optional)	2 tablespoons halved blanched almonds (optional)

Halve the melons and remove the seeds. Cut off a small amount of skin from the bottom of each melon half so that it stands level.

Whisk the egg whites and salt until stiff. Gradually whisk in the sugar until the meringue is very stiff.

Place the melon halves on a baking sheet with a scoop of ice cream in each. Spread the meringue over the ice cream and top of each melon to cover completely. Sprinkle with almonds, if using.

Cook in a preheated very hot oven (240°C/475°F, Gas Mark 9) for 2 minutes or until the meringue is golden. Serve at once.
Serves 6

Orange Ice Cream

METRIC/IMPERIAL	AMERICAN
4 eggs	4 eggs
100 g/4 oz icing sugar	1 cup confectioners sugar
300 ml/½ pint double cream	1¼ cups heavy cream
3 tablespoons honey	3 tablespoons honey
grated rind of 2 oranges	grated rind of 2 oranges
juice of 1 orange	juice of 1 orange

Separate the eggs and whisk the yolks. Whisk the egg whites separately. Gradually beat the icing sugar into the egg whites and then gradually beat in the whisked yolks.

Whip the cream until it forms soft peaks and fold it into the egg mixture with the honey and orange rind and juice.

Pour into a rigid freezerproof container and freeze for at least 2 hours. Remove from the freezer 10 minutes before serving.
Serves 4 to 6

Cottage Cheese Ice Cream

METRIC/IMPERIAL	AMERICAN
50 g/2 oz flaked almonds	½ cup sliced almonds
225 g/8 oz cottage cheese	1 cup cottage cheese
75 g/3 oz icing sugar	⅔ cup confectioners sugar
6 drops vanilla essence	6 drops vanilla
1 dessertspoon sherry	1 dessertspoon sherry
1 egg white, stiffly beaten	1 egg white, stiffly beaten

Toast the flaked almonds until just brown. Rub the cheese through a nylon sieve (strainer). Stir in the sugar, vanilla and sherry, then fold in the egg white and half the almonds.

Pour into a rigid freezerproof container and freeze until firm. Remove from the freezer 15 minutes before serving. Serve scoops or spoonfuls in individual serving dishes and sprinkle the remaining almonds on top.
Serves 6

Ginger Ice Cream

METRIC/IMPERIAL
4 egg yolks
300 ml/½ pint single
  cream
2-3 pieces stem
  ginger
4 tablespoons ginger
  syrup
300 ml/½ pint double
  cream, lightly
  whipped

AMERICAN
4 egg yolks
1¼ cups light cream
2-3 pieces preserved
  ginger
4 tablespoons ginger
  syrup
1¼ cups heavy
  cream, lightly
  whipped

Place the egg yolks in a heatproof bowl and beat until they are pale yellow and fluffy. Rinse out a small saucepan with cold water, heat the single (light) cream in the pan and slowly pour onto the egg yolks.

Place the bowl over a pan of simmering water and stir until the mixture thickens. Leave to cool.

Finely chop the ginger and add to the cooled custard with the ginger syrup. Fold in the lightly whipped cream and pour into a rigid freezerproof container. Place in the freezer until the mixture starts to set. Remove and stir through with a fork to ensure that the pieces of ginger are evenly distributed through the ice cream. Return to the freezer until firm.

Remove from the freezer one hour before serving and leave in the fridge until ready to scoop into dishes.
Serves 4 to 6

Soft Fruit Ice Cream

METRIC/IMPERIAL
300 ml/½ pint milk
2 eggs
50 g/2 oz caster sugar
300 ml/½ pint double
  cream
100 g/4 oz soft fruit
  purée
a few pieces of whole
  fruit to decorate

AMERICAN
1¼ cups milk
2 eggs
¼ cup sugar
1¼ cups heavy cream
½ cup soft fruit purée
a few pieces of whole
  fruit to decorate

Place the milk in a pan and heat gently. Beat the eggs and sugar together and gradually stir in the milk. Return the custard to the pan and heat gently, stirring constantly, until the custard just coats the back of a spoon. Do not let it boil. Leave custard until cold.

Lightly whip the cream and fold into the custard. Pour into a shallow container and freeze as quickly as possible. When just frozen, beat the ice cream until it becomes soft and smooth. Pour in the fruit purée and stir once or twice to make swirls. Return to the freezer and re-freeze.

Remove the ice cream from the freezer about 30 minutes before serving.

To serve, scoop spoonfuls into individual serving dishes and decorate with pieces of fruit.
Serves 4 to 6

Desserts For Special Occasions

Honey Charlotte Russe

METRIC/IMPERIAL	AMERICAN
150 ml/¼ pint made up lemon jelly	⅔ cup made up lemon- flavored gelatin
1 packet sponge fingers	1 package lady fingers
450 g/1 lb strawberries	1 lb strawberries
2 tablespoons lemon juice	2 tablespoons lemon juice
3 tablespoons clear honey	3 tablespoons honey
1 tablespoon powdered gelatine	1 tablespoon unflavored gelatin
2 tablespoons hot water	2 tablespoons hot water
450 ml/¾ pint double cream	2 cups heavy cream
strawberries to decorate	strawberries to decorate

Lightly oil a 1.5 litre/2½ pint (1½ quart) mould or bowl. Pour a thin layer of lemon jelly (gelatin) into the bottom and chill.

Dip the sponge fingers in the remaining jelly (gelatin) and arrange in an upright position around inside of mould, pushing the ends into the jelly (gelatin). Trim to fit and chill while making the filling.

Mash the strawberries with the lemon juice and honey. Sprinkle the gelatine on the hot water and whisk with a fork to dissolve; add to the strawberries. Whisk the cream and fold into the strawberry mixture. Pour into the mould, smooth over the surface and leave to set in the refrigerator.

Turn out the dessert, dipping the mould into hot water to loosen if necessary. Decorate with strawberries and serve.

Serves 6

Honey Charlotte Russe
(Photograph: Jif Lemon Bureau)

Raspberry and Orange Meringue

METRIC/IMPERIAL	AMERICAN
1 teaspoon cornflour	1 teaspoon cornstarch
1 teaspoon vanilla	1 teaspoon vanilla
1 teaspoon white vinegar	1 teaspoon white vinegar
3 egg whites	3 egg whites
200 g/7 oz caster sugar	⅞ cup sugar
50 g/2 oz butter	¼ cup butter
115 g/4½ oz icing sugar	1 cup confectioners sugar
grated rind of 1 orange	grated rind of 1 orange
1 teaspoon orange juice	1 teaspoon orange juice
150 ml/¼ pint double cream	⅔ cup heavy cream
225-350 g/8-12 oz fresh raspberries	½-¾ lb fresh raspberries

Blend the cornflour (cornstarch), vanilla and vinegar in a cup. Whisk the egg whites until stiff. Whisk in a little sugar then fold in the remainder with the blended cornflour (cornstarch).

Cover a baking sheet with oiled greaseproof (waxed) paper and sprinkle it with a little extra caster sugar. Spoon the meringue onto the baking sheet and spread into a circle about 3.5 cm/1½ inch thick. Cook it in a preheated cool oven (140°C/275°F, Gas Mark 1) for 1 hour. Switch off the oven and leave the meringue to cool in the oven for a further 1 hour. Remove from oven, cool and carefully tear off paper.

Cream together the butter and icing (confectioners) sugar. Add the grated orange rind and beat in the juice. Whisk the double cream until softly stiff and fold it into the butter cream. Spread this over the meringue and finally cover the top with the raspberries.

Cooking time: 1 hour
Serves 6

Special Cream Roll

METRIC/IMPERIAL	AMERICAN
4 egg yolks	4 egg yolks
175 g/6 oz caster sugar	¾ cup sugar
grated rind of 1 lemon	grated rind of 1 lemon
50 g/2 oz plain flour	½ cup all-purpose flour
6 egg whites	6 egg whites
Filling:	**Filling:**
2 tablespoons caster sugar	2 tablespoons sugar
1 teaspoon cornflour	1 teaspoon cornstarch
2 tablespoons orange juice	2 tablespoons orange juice
2 tablespoons sherry	2 tablespoons sherry
1 teaspoon brandy	1 teaspoon brandy
1 egg yolk	1 egg yolk
Topping:	**Topping:**
300 ml/½ pint double cream	1¼ cups heavy cream
1 tablespoon brandy	1 tablespoon brandy
1 tablespoon apricot jam	1 tablespoon apricot jam
1 tablespoon flaked almonds, toasted	1 tablespoon sliced almonds, toasted

Beat the egg yolks until thick, then gradually beat in the sugar until the mixture is smooth. Stir the lemon rind into the flour, then fold the flour into the egg mixture. Stiffly whisk the egg whites then fold them into the mixture, one-third at a time, until all the whites are used.

Spread the mixture evenly in a greased and lined 30 × 20 cm/12 × 8 inch Swiss roll tin (jelly pan). Cook in a preheated moderately hot oven (190°C/375°F, Gas Mark 5) for 15 minutes or until the sponge springs back when touched. Turn the sponge onto a piece of greaseproof (waxed) paper sprinkled with a little extra caster sugar. Leave to cool and then peel off the lining paper.

To make the filling: mix the sugar and cornflour (cornstarch) in a bowl over a pan of boiling water and gradually stir in the orange juice, sherry, brandy and egg yolk. Continue stirring until the mixture is smooth and thick. Leave until cold. Spread the filling over the sponge and roll it up like a Swiss (jelly) roll.

Whip the cream with the brandy and jam. Spread it over the sponge roll and sprinkle with the almonds.

Serves 6

Orange and Almond Soufflé

METRIC/IMPERIAL	AMERICAN
3 large eggs, separated	3 large eggs, separated
175 g/6 oz caster sugar	¾ cup sugar
grated rind of 1 lemon	grated rind of 1 lemon
grated rind and juice of 3 oranges	grated rind and juice of 3 oranges
15 g/½ oz powdered gelatine	2 tablespoons unflavored gelatin
juice of ½ lemon, made up to 75 ml/ 2½ fl oz with water	juice of ½ lemon, made up to ⅓ cup with water
300 ml/½ pint orange yogurt	1¼ cups orange yogurt
few drops almond essence	few drops almond extract
To decorate:	**To decorate:**
2 tablespoons crushed macaroon crumbs	2 tablespoons crushed macaroon crumbs
whipped double cream	whipped heavy cream
few halved almonds, browned	few halved almonds, browned
1 peeled and sliced orange	1 peeled and sliced orange

Tie a band of double greaseproof (waxed) paper round a 15 cm/6 inch soufflé dish to stand 2.5 cm/1 inch above the rim of the dish.

Place the egg yolks, sugar, lemon and orange rinds and orange juice in a heatproof basin over a pan of simmering water. Whisk until the mixture is quite thick. Remove from the heat and continue whisking until the bowl is cool.

Sprinkle the gelatine over the lemon juice and water in a bowl over a pan of simmering water and stir until dissolved. Leave to cool.

Fold the yogurt and almond essence (extract) into the whisked mixture, then fold in the gelatine. Put the mixture into the refrigerator until it is on the point of setting.

Whisk the egg whites until stiff and fold into the soufflé mixture. Pour into the soufflé dish and return to the refrigerator until completely set.

Carefully peel off the paper band. Press the macaroon crumbs gently round the sides. Decorate the top with rosettes of whipped cream, almonds and the orange slices.

Serves 4 to 6

Chocolate and Raspberry Gâteau

METRIC/IMPERIAL	AMERICAN
4 eggs	4 eggs
100 g/4 oz caster sugar	½ cup sugar
75 g/3 oz plain flour	¾ cup all-purpose flour
5 tablespoons cocoa powder	5 tablespoons sweetened cocoa
Filling and decoration:	**Filling and decoration:**
225 g/8 oz plain chocolate	8 squares (1 oz each) semi-sweet chocolate
300 ml/½ pint double cream	1¼ cups heavy cream
350 g/12 oz fresh raspberries	¾ lb fresh raspberries

Place the eggs and sugar in a large heatproof basin over a pan of hot water and whisk until the mixture is thick and pale. Remove from the heat and whisk for a further minute. (If using an electric beater, the hot water is not necessary.)

Sift the flour and cocoa and gently fold into the egg mixture. Spoon into a greased 20 cm/8 inch loose-bottomed cake tin (spring-form pan) and spread evenly. Cook in a preheated moderate oven (180°C/350°F, Gas Mark 4) for 40 to 50 minutes until well risen and firm to the touch. Leave in the tin (pan) for 5 minutes before turning out onto a wire rack to cool completely. Split the cake into three horizontal layers.

Melt the chocolate in a basin over a pan of hot water and spread half of the chocolate over the top layer of cake. Leave to set. Spread the remaining chocolate thinly on a piece of lightly oiled foil or non-stick paper (parchment) and leave to set. Cut into 3.5 cm/1½ inch squares with a sharp knife and peel off the foil.

Whisk the cream until thick and spread or pipe three-quarters of the cream over the remaining two layers of cake. Reserve some of the raspberries for decoration and place the remaining raspberries on top of the cream and sandwich the layers of cake together with the chocolate-covered layer on top. Pipe whirls of cream on top of the cake and decorate with the chocolate squares and remaining raspberries.
Cooking time: 1 hour
Serves 6 to 8

Strawberry Shortcake

METRIC/IMPERIAL	AMERICAN
225 g/8 oz plain flour	2 cups all-purpose flour
pinch of salt	pinch of salt
4 teaspoons baking powder	4 teaspoons baking powder
75 g/3 oz butter	6 tablespoons butter
1 large egg	1 large egg
40 g/1½ oz caster sugar	3 tablespoons sugar
3 tablespoons milk	3 tablespoons milk
1 tablespoon melted butter	1 tablespoon melted butter
Filling:	**Filling:**
1 tablespoon custard powder	1 tablespoon Bird's English Dessert Mix
300 ml/½ pint milk	1¼ cups milk
2 tablespoons sugar	2 tablespoons sugar
150 ml/¼ pint double cream	⅔ cup heavy cream
450 g/1 lb fresh or frozen and thawed strawberries	1 lb fresh or frozen and thawed strawberries
8 whole almonds, toasted	8 whole almonds, toasted

Mix the flour, salt and baking powder in a bowl. Rub (cut) in the butter. Lightly mix the egg, sugar and milk together and pour into the centre of the dry ingredients. Mix to a rough dough using a fork. Turn onto a floured surface and knead to form a smooth dough. Divide in half.

Shape each half into a circle to fit a 20 cm/8 inch sandwich tin (layer cake pan). Put one circle in the tin (pan), brush with the melted butter and place the second circle on top.

Cook in a preheated hot oven (220°C/425°F, Gas Mark 7) for 20 to 25 minutes until risen and golden. Cool slightly, then separate the two halves.

Make up the custard (Dessert Mix) using the milk and sugar. Whisk until smooth. Cover and leave to cool.

Whip the cream until just stiff. Reserve about 2 tablespoons cream for decoration and fold the remaining cream into the custard.

Reserve one-third of the custard mixture and eight strawberries for the top. Halve remaining strawberries and mix into the custard mixture. Spread over one shortcake round. Cover with the second layer of shortcake. Spread the top with the reserved custard mixture.

Decorate with the whole strawberries, reserved cream and almonds.
Serves 6

Chocolate Peppermint Gâteau

METRIC/IMPERIAL	AMERICAN
150 g/5 oz self-raising flour	1¼ cups self-rising flour
25 g/1 oz cocoa powder	¼ cup unsweetened cocoa
2 bars peppermint Aero	2 peppermint candy bars
3 tablespoons milk	3 tablespoons milk
175 g/6 oz margarine	¾ cup margarine
175 g/6 oz caster sugar	¾ cup sugar
3 eggs, beaten	3 eggs, beaten
Filling:	**Filling:**
450 ml/¾ pint double cream	2 cups heavy cream
1-3 teaspoons peppermint essence	1-3 teaspoons peppermint extract
To decorate:	**To decorate:**
2 bars peppermint Aero	2 peppermint candy bars
1 box After Eight Mints	1 box chocolate after dinner mints (wafer thin)

Mix together the flour and cocoa. Break up the two peppermint bars and melt them in the milk in a basin over a pan of hot water. Leave on one side to cool.

Cream together the margarine and sugar until light and fluffy. Gradually beat in the eggs with a little of the flour and cocoa. Stir in the melted chocolate and milk mixture, then fold in the remaining flour and cocoa.

Divide the mixture between two 20 cm/8 inch greased sandwich tins (layer cake pans) and cook in a preheated moderately hot oven (190°C/375°F, Gas Mark 5) for about 25 minutes. Turn cakes onto a wire rack and leave to cool.

Whip the cream and add peppermint essence (extract) to taste.

Cut the two sponge cakes in half horizontally. Sandwich the four layers together using about two-thirds of the peppermint cream. Spread a little more of the peppermint cream around the sides of the cake.

Melt the remaining peppermint bars in a basin over a pan of hot water. Spread the melted chocolate over the top of the cake. Decorate the sides of the cake by pressing after dinner mints onto the cream. Pipe whirls of remaining cream around the top edge of the cake and place half an after dinner mint (cut in the shape of a triangle) between each whirl.
Cooking time: 35 minutes
Serves 8 to 10

Creamy Peach Gâteau

METRIC/IMPERIAL	AMERICAN
3 eggs	3 eggs
6 tablespoons caster sugar	6 tablespoons sugar
75 g/3 oz plain flour	¾ cup all-purpose flour
50 g/2 oz butter, melted	¼ cup butter, melted
few drops vanilla essence	few drops vanilla
1 × 425 g/15 oz can sliced peaches	1 × 15 oz can sliced peaches
300 ml/½ pint double cream, whipped	1¼ cups heavy cream, whipped
100 g/4 oz ratafia biscuits	¼ lb ratafia biscuits
few angelica leaves to decorate	few angelica leaves to decorate

Place the eggs and sugar in a large bowl and whisk until thick and creamy. Carefully fold in the flour. Warm the butter slightly, then quickly fold into the mixture with the vanilla. Divide the mixture between two greased and lined 18 cm/7 inch sandwich tins (layer cake pans). Cook in a preheated moderately hot oven (200°C/400°F, Gas Mark 6) for 20 to 25 minutes. Cool on a wire rack.

Drain the peaches, reserving the syrup. Spoon the syrup over the cold sponge cakes and leave to soak.

Chop one quarter of the peach slices and mix with a little of the whipped cream. Sandwich the two sponge cakes together with the peach and cream mixture. Spread some cream around the sides of the gâteau.

Press the biscuits onto the sides until completely covered. Pipe or spread a little more of the cream on top of the gâteau, then decorate with the remaining peach slices and angelica leaves. Spoon the remaining cream into a piping (pastry) bag fitted with a large star nozzle and pipe cream around the top edge of the gâteau.

Chill before serving.
Cooking time: 25 minutes
Serves 6 to 8

Chocolate Peppermint Gâteau; Creamy Peach Gâteau; Viennese Mandarin Slice (page 60)
(Photograph: The Homepride Kitchen)

Chocolate Pear Flan

METRIC/IMPERIAL	AMERICAN
75 g/3 oz butter	6 tablespoons butter
225 g/8 oz plain chocolate wholemeal biscuits, crushed	3 cups graham cracker crumbs
2 × 415 g/14½ oz cans pear halves	2 × 16 oz cans pear halves
2 teaspoons arrowroot	2 teaspoons arrowroot
grated chocolate to decorate	grated chocolate to decorate

Melt the butter in a pan. Remove from the heat, add the crushed biscuits and stir well.

Press the crumbs into the base and up the sides of an 18 cm/7 inch loose-bottomed fluted flan tin (pie pan). Place in the refrigerator to set. When quite firm, carefully remove the crumb case from the tin, leaving it on the base for easier serving.

Drain the pears reserving the juice and arrange them in the flan (pie). Blend the arrowroot with half of the juice in a pan and bring gently to the boil, stirring until the mixture thickens and clears. Cool a little and pour over the pears.

When cold, sprinkle with the grated chocolate. Serve with cream.
Serves 6

Fridge Cake

METRIC/IMPERIAL	AMERICAN
1 packet trifle sponge cakes	1 package individual dessert sponge shells
100 g/4 oz plain chocolate	4 squares (1 oz each) semi-sweet chocolate
4 tablespoons milk	4 tablespoons milk
4 egg yolks	4 egg yolks
100 g/4 oz caster sugar	½ cup sugar
1 teaspoon strong black coffee	1 teaspoon strong black coffee
300 ml/½ pint double cream	1¼ cups heavy cream
grated chocolate to decorate	grated chocolate to decorate

Line a 1.2 litre/2 pint (5 cup) loaf tin (pan) with foil. Cut the sponges into thick slices and use some to line sides and bottom of loaf tin (pan).

Melt the chocolate in a basin over a pan of hot water. Stir in the milk.

Whisk the egg yolks and sugar in a basin over a pan of hot water and add the chocolate mixture. Whisk until the mixture thickens. Remove from the heat and add the coffee.

Place alternate layers of sponge slices and chocolate mixture in the tin (pan), finishing with a layer of cake. Chill for 12 hours.

Whip the cream and spoon into a piping (pastry) bag fitted with a star nozzle. Pipe the cream over cake and decorate with chocolate.
Serves 6 to 8

Viennese Mandarin Slice

METRIC/IMPERIAL	AMERICAN
225 g/8 oz margarine	1 cup margarine
50 g/2 oz caster sugar	¼ cup sugar
1 teaspoon vanilla essence	1 teaspoon vanilla
225 g/8 oz plain flour	2 cups all-purpose flour
Filling and topping:	**Filling and topping:**
1 × 312 g/11 oz can mandarin orange segments, drained	1 × 11 oz can mandarin orange segments, drained
300 ml/½ pint double cream, whipped	1¼ cups heavy cream, whipped
25 g/1 oz flaked almonds, browned	¼ cup sliced almonds, browned

Cream together the margarine and sugar until light and fluffy, then beat in the vanilla. Gradually fold in the flour. Spoon the mixture into a piping (pastry) bag fitted with a large star nozzle. Pipe 14 "fingers", each 7.5 cm/3 inches in length, close together, side by side onto a greased baking sheet. Repeat twice more to make three rectangles all the same size.

Cook in a preheated moderately hot oven (200°C/400°F, Gas Mark 6) for about 20 minutes until golden brown. Cool on wire racks.

To prepare the filling: chop half of the mandarin oranges and mix with two-thirds of the whipped cream.

Carefully lift one shortcake rectangle onto a long serving plate. Spread over half of the cream and orange mixture. Place another shortcake rectangle on top, spread with the remaining cream and orange mixture. Place the third shortcake slice on top.

Spoon the remaining cream into a piping (pastry) bag fitted with a star nozzle and pipe the cream around the top edges. Decorate with rows of mandarin oranges and almonds.
Cooking time: 20 minutes
Serves 6 to 8
Illustrated on page 59

60

Cherry Gâteau

METRIC/IMPERIAL	AMERICAN
100 g/4 oz unsalted butter	½ cup unsalted butter
100 g/4 oz caster sugar	½ cup sugar
2 eggs	2 eggs
100 g/4 oz self-raising flour	1 cup self-rising flour
1 tablespoon cocoa powder	1 tablespoon sweetened cocoa
1 tablespoon warm water	1 tablespoon warm water
1 × 425 g/15 oz can black cherries	1 × 15 oz can bing cherries
2 teaspoons cornflour	2 teaspoons cornstarch
300 ml/½ pint double cream	1¼ cups heavy cream
2 tablespoons cherry liqueur (optional)	2 tablespoons cherry liqueur (optional)

Cream the butter and sugar until light and fluffy. Beat in the eggs. Sift together the flour and cocoa and fold into the creamed mixture. Stir in the water. Divide the mixture between two greased 18 cm/7 inch sandwich tins (layer cake pans).

Cook in a preheated moderate oven (180°C/350°F, Gas Mark 4) for about 25 minutes or until firm to the touch. Turn out onto a wire rack after 10 minutes and leave until cold.

Drain the cherries, reserving the juice. Reserve a few cherries for decoration, stone (pit) and chop the remainder of them. Mix the cornflour (cornstarch) with a little of the cherry juice. Heat the remaining juice, pour onto the cornflour (cornstarch) mixture and then return to the pan and stir until thickened. Remove from the heat, add the chopped cherries and leave until cold. Whip the cream until thick.

Soak the cakes with the cherry liqueur, if using. Spread the cherry mixture over one half of the cake and spread one-third of the cream over the cherries. Cover with the other cake. Spread another third of the cream over the top of the cake. Pipe the remaining cream in rosettes around top of cake and decorate with the whole cherries.

Cooking time: 30 minutes
Serves 6

Glitter Flan

METRIC/IMPERIAL	AMERICAN
100 g/4 oz butter, softened	½ cup butter, softened
50 g/2 oz caster sugar	¼ cup sugar
175 g/6 oz plain flour	1½ cups all-purpose flour
Filling and sauce:	**Filling and sauce:**
1 teaspoon cornflour	1 teaspoon cornstarch
½ teaspoon ground cinnamon	½ teaspoon ground cinnamon
150 ml/¼ pint milk, made with dried milk powder	⅔ cup milk, made with dried milk powder
1 tablespoon sugar	1 tablespoon sugar
2 egg yolks	2 egg yolks
150 ml/¼ pint plain yogurt	⅔ cup plain yogurt
150 ml/¼ pint strawberry yogurt	⅔ cup strawberry yogurt
1 × 275 g/10 oz can strawberries	1 × 10 oz can strawberries
25 g/1 oz flaked almonds	¼ cup sliced almonds
2 tablespoons demerara sugar	2 tablespoons brown sugar

Cream the butter and sugar together. Fold in the flour to make a fairly stiff dough. Press this into a 20 cm/8 inch flan (pie) dish to cover the sides and bottom evenly. Prick the bottom, line with greaseproof (waxed) paper and dried beans and bake in a preheated moderately hot oven (190°C/375°F, Gas Mark 5) for 10 minutes. Remove the paper and beans and bake for a further 15 minutes. Leave to cool in the dish while preparing the filling.

Blend the cornflour (cornstarch) and cinnamon with a little milk in a pan, then stir in the remaining milk and bring to the boil to thicken. Stir in the sugar and, when cooled slightly, pour this custard onto the egg yolks, stirring well. Add the yogurts and pour into the flan (pie) case.

Drain the juice from the strawberries and reserve. Arrange the strawberries over the top of the flan. Cook in a preheated moderately hot oven (190°C/375°F, Gas Mark 5) for 30 to 40 minutes until lightly set. Cover with foil if it browns. Remove from the oven. Mix the almonds and sugar together, sprinkle on top and quickly brown under the grill for a minute.

If liked, heat the reserved juice, thicken with a little blended cornflour (cornstarch) and serve as a sauce with the flan.

Cooking time: 1 hour
Serves 6 to 8

Fresh and Fruity

METRIC/IMPERIAL	AMERICAN
450 g/1 lb plums or damsons, halved and stoned	1 lb plums or damsons, halved and pitted
2 tablespoons water	2 tablespoons water
450 ml/¾ pint milk	2 cups milk
few drops vanilla essence	few drops vanilla
3 eggs	3 eggs
1 egg yolk	1 egg yolk
1 tablespoon sugar	1 tablespoon sugar
To decorate:	**To decorate:**
whipped cream	whipped cream
toasted almonds	toasted almonds

Place the fruit in a pan with the water and some sugar to taste. Cover and simmer gently until the fruit is tender. Put half the fruit into the base of a 1.2 litre/2 pint (5 cup) ovenproof dish.

Warm the milk with the vanilla in a pan. Lightly beat the eggs, egg yolk and sugar, pour in the milk and mix together. Strain the egg and milk mixture and very gently pour it over the fruit in the dish. Cover with foil.

Put the dish into a roasting tin with enough cold water to come halfway up the sides of the dish. Cook in a preheated moderate oven (160°C/325°F, Gas Mark 3) for 50 to 60 minutes or until the custard has set. Cool, then refrigerate until cold.

Carefully spread the remaining fruit over the custard and top with whipped cream and almonds.
Cooking time: 1 hour
Serves 4

Soufflé Mirabelle

METRIC/IMPERIAL	AMERICAN
100 g/4 oz plain chocolate	4 squares (1 oz each) semi-sweet chocolate
300 ml/½ pint milk	1¼ cups milk
50 g/2 oz caster sugar	¼ cup sugar
few drops vanilla essence	few drops vanilla
3 eggs, separated	3 eggs, separated
4 teaspoons powdered gelatine	4 teaspoons unflavored gelatin
2 tablespoons hot water	2 tablespoons hot water
300 ml/½ pint double cream	1¼ cups heavy cream
100 g/4 oz toffee brittle, crushed	¼ lb toffee brittle, crushed

Tie a band of double greaseproof (waxed) paper around a 15 cm/6 inch soufflé dish to stand 5 cm/2 inches above the rim; oil the inside of the paper.

Grate the chocolate into a pan and add the milk, sugar and vanilla. Heat very gently. Stir the egg yolks into the chocolate sauce and reheat but do not boil. Leave to cool.

Dissolve the gelatine in the hot water and stir it into the chocolate sauce. Whip the cream and fold it in, reserving some for decoration. Whisk egg whites until stiff, then fold into the mixture.

Pour the mixture into the prepared soufflé dish and leave to set.

Carefully remove the paper collar. Decorate with remainder of cream and toffee brittle.
Serves 4 to 6

Orange and Lemon Cheesecake

METRIC/IMPERIAL	AMERICAN
200 g/7 oz soft cream cheese	⅞ cup soft cream cheese
150 ml/¼ pint soured cream	⅔ cup sour cream
100 g/4 oz caster sugar	½ cup sugar
½ teaspoon vanilla essence	½ teaspoon vanilla
1 packet lemon jelly	1 package lemon-flavored gelatin
150 ml/¼ pint hot water	⅔ cup hot water
50 g/2 oz unsalted butter	¼ cup unsalted butter
100 g/4 oz digestive biscuits, crushed	1½ cups graham cracker crumbs
150 ml/¼ pint double cream	⅔ cup heavy cream
mandarin orange segments to decorate	mandarin orange segments to decorate

Cream the cheese. Add the sour cream, sugar and vanilla. Dissolve the jelly (gelatin) in the hot water and allow to cool slightly.

Melt the butter in a pan and stir in the biscuit (cracker) crumbs. Press the crumb mixture into the bottom of a 20 cm/8 inch loose-bottomed cake tin (springform pan).

Whip the cream until fairly thick and mix it into the cream cheese mixture. Fold in the lemon jelly (gelatin). Pour the mixture into the cake tin (pan). Leave in the refrigerator to set.

Just before serving, remove from the tin and decorate top with drained mandarin oranges.
Serves 6 to 8

Index

The publishers wish to acknowledge the following photographers: Robert Golden: cover. Paul Williams: page 2. Alan Duns: pages 46 and 54.

Recipes for this book have been contributed by the following companies: Ambrosia Rice; The British Egg Information Service; The Cadbury Typhoo Food Advisory Service; Canned Food Advisory Service; Carmel Produce Information Bureau; Corning Housewares Information Centre; The Danish Food Centre, London; Davis Gelatine Information Service; The Dutch Dairy Bureau; Flour Advisory Bureau; Fyffes Group Ltd; Gales Honey Bureau; The Home-pride Kitchen: John West Foods; National Dairy Council; Outline Slimming Bureau; The Rice Information Bureau.

PDO 82-0163